TEACHING WITH CLASSROOM RESPONSE SYSTEMS

D1039927

TEACHING WITH CLASSROOM RESPONSE SYSTEMS

Creating Active Learning Environments

Derek Bruff

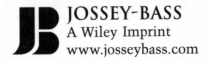

JOSSEY-BASS
A Wiley Imprint
www.josseybass.com

Published by Jossey-Bass
A Wiley Imprint
989 Market Street, San Francisco, CA 94103-1741—www.josseybass.com

Readers should be aware that Internet Web sites offered as citations and/or sources for further information may have changed or disappeared between the time this was written and when it is read.

Limit of Liability/Disclaimer of Warranty: While the publisher and author have used their best efforts in preparing this book, they make no representations or warranties with respect to the accuracy or completeness of the contents of this book and specifically disclaim any implied warranties of merchantability or fitness for a particular purpose. No warranty may be created or extended by sales representatives or written sales materials. The advice and strategies contained herein may not be suitable for your situation. You should consult with a professional where appropriate. Neither the publisher nor author shall be liable for any loss of profit or any other commercial damages, including but not limited to special, incidental, consequential, or other damages.

Jossey-Bass books and products are available through most bookstores. To contact Jossey-Bass directly call our Customer Care Department within the U.S. at 800-956-7739, outside the U.S. at 317-572-3986, or fax 317-572-4002.

Jossey-Bass also publishes its books in a variety of electronic formats. Some content that appears in print may not be available in electronic books.
Example 3.3 on page 78 copyright Eric Mazur.

Library of Congress Cataloging-in-Publication Data

Bruff, Derek.
    Teaching with classroom response systems : creating active learning environments / Derek Bruff.—1st ed.
        p. cm.—(The Jossey-Bass higher and adult education series)
    Includes bibliographical references and index.
    ISBN 978-0-470-28893-1 (pbk.)
    1. Active learning. 2. Simulated environment (Teaching method) 3. Teaching—Aids and devices. I. Title.
    LB1027.23.B78 2009
    371.39—dc22

                        2008043433

Printed in the United States of America

FIRST EDITION
PB Printing 10 9 8 7 6 5 4 3 2 1

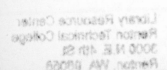

The Jossey-Bass

Higher and Adult Education Series

Contents

To my wife, Amy, and daughters, Sophie and Lucy

PREFACE

I first learned about classroom response systems during a talk by Harvard University physics professor Eric Mazur at Vanderbilt University. I had taught several mathematics courses and had experimented with a variety of teaching methods designed to promote active learning among my students. When Mazur described his use of classroom response systems to facilitate what he called peer instruction—posing a question to his students and having them discuss it in pairs and submit their answers using handheld devices called "clickers"—I knew I wanted to try this technique in my teaching. It fit well with my teaching philosophy, and it seemed to have great potential for engaging students during class and providing me information about their learning that I could use to teach more effectively.

I had the chance to use clickers while teaching in the Harvard University mathematics department. That first semester I was fortunate to have a set of calculus questions developed by Maria Terrell's GoodQuestions project at Cornell University. The following semester, I started writing my own linear algebra questions. The technology was difficult to use then. Before every class session, I picked up a very old computer on a large computer cart from the basement and wheeled it onto the elevator and up to my classroom. The system my colleagues and I used relied on infrared frequencies, which meant that the clickers the students used needed to have line of sight with the receiver. As a result, our receiver was mounted on a six-foot-tall wood plank nailed to the side of the computer cart. At the start of each class session, my students picked up clickers from a box and returned them to the box at the end of the class. In spite of the challenges, I was hooked. The classroom response system and the peer instruction teaching method delivered on the promise I had seen in Mazur's presentation.

Since those first semesters teaching with clickers, I have made classroom response systems a regular part of my mathematics teaching. Through my work at the Vanderbilt University Center for Teaching, I consult regularly with instructors at Vanderbilt and elsewhere about their use of clickers. Hearing from instructors in other disciplines about their experiences teaching with clickers has shown me that this instructional technology can be used in a variety of ways to transform classroom dynamics. A couple of years ago, I saw the need for a practical guide to teaching with clickers that instructors could use to learn about ways they might use clickers in their teaching, and I decided to write one. I have enjoyed sharing examples of clicker questions and activities in various consultation, workshop, and conference settings during the past few years, and I hope that readers will find this book to be full of great ideas and inspiration for using clickers effectively in their own classrooms.

INTRODUCTION TO THIS BOOK

This book is intended to be a practical guide for instructors interested in teaching with classroom response systems. The book features descriptions and examples of activities that make good use of these systems—activities that engage students in course material and provide feedback on student learning useful to both students and instructors. The book also features descriptions and examples of types of multiple-choice questions instructors frequently use with classroom response systems, as well as discussions of many of the common instructional, technical, and logistical challenges that can arise in teaching with this technology.

The focus throughout the book is more on teaching than on technology. The technology used in classroom response systems is constantly changing, so any discussion of using clickers that relies on features of current technologies is likely to be out of date soon. Another reason is that research indicates that the effectiveness of classroom response systems depends largely on the ways in which instructors use these systems—the kinds of questions they ask and the ways they use clickers to structure classroom activities. Thus, this book assumes very little about the specific technologies of classroom response systems other than the following relatively abstract description. Instructors pose questions, usually multiple-choice questions, to their students; students submit answers using handheld response devices; and the system generates a bar chart showing the distribution of student responses. Technology may change—students might in the future respond using cell phones with wireless Internet connections instead of today's clicker devices, for instance—but the fundamental uses of these systems for engaging and assessing students are not likely to change. One consequence of this focus on teaching is that the teaching methods described here should apply to any instructor using a classroom response system, regardless of the brand of system used. Another is that no currently available systems are mentioned by name.

The book's goal is not to tell instructors how they should or should not use classroom response systems. Each instructor's choices regarding how to use these systems depend on his or her teaching goals and context. A type of question or a structure for a classroom activity that uses clickers might work well for one instructor, but not as well for another instructor teaching a different kind of course in a different discipline to different students. Thus, the discussion of classroom response systems in this book focuses on the many choices instructors have when using these systems, exploring the advantages and disadvantages of each choice. For example, if an instructor decides to include clicker questions as part of students' course grades, should full credit be given to all student responses or only to correct ones? Either choice poses trade-offs, ones that are explored in Chapter Four. The choice any individual instructor makes depends on many factors: the learning goals the instructor has for the students, the ways in which the instructor's students are motivated to engage in course material, the nature of learning in the instructor's discipline, and so on. The discussion of teaching choices in this book is meant to help instructors make informed and intentional decisions about their use of clickers in the light of those factors.

In order to explore the many ways instructors use classroom response systems, almost fifty instructors in different disciplines at different types of institutions were interviewed in the process of researching this book. I asked about the kinds of questions they use with clickers, the ways they use clickers to structure classroom activities and discussion, the challenges they have faced when using this technology, and the responses their students have had to learning in this way. Each instructor's teaching context is different, and the stories and sample questions drawn from these interviews show the many different choices instructors make given their disciplines, their courses, and their students. These instructors' experiences and perspectives help make more concrete the ideas and strategies for teaching with clickers discussed here. Many instructors appreciate hearing how their peers and colleagues implement teaching methods and strategies. The examples drawn from these interviews should provide readers with inspiration for their own classrooms.

Although classroom response systems are frequently used in elementary and secondary education, the teaching context explored in this book is that of postsecondary education at colleges and universities. Most of the examples in the book are drawn from undergraduate settings, although several professional fields, including law, nursing, veterinary medicine, and pharmacy, are represented as well. Teachers in elementary and secondary education settings interested in teaching with clickers will likely find much of value in this book, although some of the ideas and strategies presented here might not translate well from the postsecondary contexts to K–12 settings. (For insight into how clickers are used in K–12 settings, see Penuel, Boscardin, Masyn, and Crawford, 2007, who share the results of a survey of almost five hundred elementary and secondary educators.) Given the focus on postsecondary education, the term *instructor* is used throughout this book as an inclusive term to describe those who teach in higher education settings. Not all who teach in these settings are faculty members; some are staff members and graduate students. The term *instructor* is meant to include all of these groups. Although *teacher* is an accurate descriptor as well, its K–12 connotation makes *instructor* a somewhat more appropriate term given the intended audience of this book.

Chapter One explores several ways in which classroom response systems can be used to engage students in the learning process. Engaged students are those who actively and intentionally participate during class, giving serious thought to the topics discussed. Frequently students become engaged during small-group and classwide discussions, and Chapter One describes several ways clickers can be used to facilitate these discussions. One structure for doing so is called peer instruction, which involves posing a clicker question and having students discuss it in pairs or small groups before submitting their answers using clickers. A number of frequently asked questions about peer instruction are discussed in Chapter One.

Chapter Two focuses on the various ways the information about student learning provided by classroom response systems can be used to tailor instruction to the learning needs of students. Since clickers allow instructors to assess their students' learning and hear their students' perspectives several times in a class session, these systems provide information that is useful in making on-the-spot teaching decisions. Some instructors find this kind of agile teaching daunting, so Chapter Two includes suggested answers to many frequently asked questions about this approach to leveraging the results of clicker questions. The chapter also discusses the uses of clickers to facilitate graded quizzes and tests. Many instructors use clickers for this purpose, in part because it allows them to provide their students with more timely feedback on their learning.

Although the ways in which instructors use clickers in the classroom are key to their effectiveness, also important are the clicker questions themselves. Chapter Three sets out many sample questions drawn from the interviews conducted for this book. Most instructors use clickers to ask various kinds of content questions—questions asking students to recall information, demonstrate understanding of a concept, apply concepts or techniques to specific problems or situations, or think critically about difficult topics. These types of questions are explored, as are process questions used to shape students' classroom learning experiences. These latter questions include those asking about student opinions and experiences, those asking students to assess their confidence in answering content questions, those that monitor various aspects of students' learning processes, and those designed to facilitate the kinds of classroom experiments often conducted in social science courses.

Invariably when instructors start thinking about the use of clickers in their courses, a number of questions occur to them.

The next two chapters provide possible answers to many of these questions. The questions discussed in Chapter Four deal with the teaching choices instructors using clickers face: how to balance active learning and covering content in class sessions, how to write effective clicker questions, how to respond to students who resist participating in clicker questions, whether and how to grade clicker questions, and how to manage the process of asking and sharing the results of clicker questions. Chapter Four also includes a discussion of the uses of clickers in small courses—uses that are sometimes very different from those in large-enrollment courses. The questions in Chapter Five explore technical and logistical aspects of classroom response systems: questions about learning the technology, selecting a classroom response system vendor, supporting and promoting the use of clickers, low-tech alternatives to clickers such as hand-raising and response card methods, and high-tech clickers such as student laptops and cell phones.

The book concludes in Chapter Six with a summary of reasons for using classroom response systems. The ability of a system to collect and display responses from all of the students in a class session can increase student participation and engagement and improve the learning process by making student learning difficulties and student perspectives more visible. These and other reasons to use clickers are explored in this chapter, which ends with sixteen concrete suggestions for instructors interested in using clickers.

Instructors completely new to teaching with clickers are advised to read Chapters One through Three first to get a sense of the variety of question types and activities frequently used with clickers, as well as the section on getting started in Chapter Five. Instructors already employing teaching methods designed to promote active learning and provide feedback on student learning will likely find that the activities and questions described in these chapters fit well with their current teaching practices. Instructors not already using such methods will find in these chapters ways to start integrating clickers in their teaching in small but meaningful ways. Some instructors find that clickers completely transform their teaching in productive ways, but others find ways to enhance what they are already doing with selective applications of classroom response systems.

Those already using classroom response systems in their teaching primarily for assessment might also start in Chapter One to learn about ways of expanding their teaching practice to use clickers for engaging students in learning. Current clicker users might also find useful Chapter Three for helping them write more effective clicker questions and Chapter Four for helping them think about teaching choices they might not have considered.

Another segment of the intended audience consists of faculty and staff who support instructors in their use of clickers, particularly those who provide instructional design and development support. These readers will find many effective ways to use clickers that they can share with the instructors with whom they work. They will also likely find the logistical and technical questions discussed in Chapter Five particularly useful.

Finally, all instructors reading this book are encouraged to look throughout the book for examples from the interviews that are relevant to their own or similar disciplines or to their institutional settings. Potential uses and advantages of teaching with clickers often become clearer to instructors when they can see how colleagues teaching similar courses or similar students use clickers. Although not every discipline is represented in this book, examples drawn from the humanities, the natural sciences and engineering, the social sciences, and several professional fields are included. Readers should be able to find inspiration for their own use of clickers in the many examples described here.

ACKNOWLEDGMENTS

After leading a few workshops on clickers, I realized how important it is for instructors to hear their peers' and colleagues' experiences before trying a new instructional technique. As a result, I began interviewing instructors in different disciplines and at different kinds of institutions about their experiences teaching with clickers. Their experiences inform this book, and readers will find their stories throughout the chapters. I thank these instructors for their time and for sharing their creative and effective uses of classroom response systems: Bruce Atwood, Brian Augustine, Robert Bartsch, Stuart Beatty, Thomas Benzing, Meagan Bowler, Corly Brooke, Mary Burke, Teresa Cosby, Anthony Crider, Elizabeth Cullingford, Marcie Desrochers,

Michael Dorsher, Weston Dripps, Francisco Estrada-Belli, Parvanak Fassihi, Brian Fitzpatrick, Rafael Gely, Charlene Harkins, Kristen Hessler, Bill Hill, Angel Hoekstra, Shane Hutson, Dennis Jacobs, Linda Johnston, Stacy Klein, Karina Kline-Gabel, Philippa Levine, Adam List, Margaret Logan, Adam Lucas, Ron McClamrock, Meredeth McCoy, Matthew Mulvaney, Teri J. Murphy, Thomas Palmeri, Lori Paluti, Steven Pollock, Barbara Reisner, Adam Rich, Michael Richman, Edna Ross, Ivan Shibley, Kori Street, Amanda Tapler, Resa Walch, and Yaoling Wang. Thanks also to the many instructors not listed here with whom I have talked informally about clickers, including my colleagues at Vanderbilt and elsewhere.

Thanks also to my colleagues at the Center for Teaching for their support during the process of writing this book. Particular thanks go to Allison Pingree for encouraging me to write a book on clickers. Thanks also to James Anker for his interest in this project and support during its initial stages and to Steven Gilbert and Stephen Ehrmann for great conversations about clickers and the chance to share my ideas with a wider audience. I also thank my mathematics colleagues—Matthew Leingang, Kelly Cline, Holly Zullo, and Mark Parker—for helping me talk about clickers with the mathematics community and my colleagues in the instructional development community, particularly Peter Felten, Kate Brinko, Katie Kearns, and Paul Quick, for their support and encouragement as I pursued my research on clickers, as well as those who introduced me to instructors whom I interviewed. Thanks also to all of my other colleagues who have helped with this project whom I have not mentioned here.

Thanks especially to my wife, Amy, and our daughters, Sophie and Lucy, for their patience, encouragement, and love.

DEREK BRUFF

THE AUTHOR

Derek Bruff is an assistant director at the Vanderbilt University Center for Teaching and a senior lecturer in the Vanderbilt University Department of Mathematics. Prior to his current position, he was a faculty preceptor in the Harvard University Department of Mathematics, teaching several courses and coordinating multi-section calculus courses. He earned a Ph.D. in mathematics from Vanderbilt University.

Bruff's primary research interests center on investigating effective uses of classroom response systems. To that end, he consults regularly with instructors in a variety of disciplines at Vanderbilt and elsewhere about teaching with clickers, offers workshops for instructors on clickers at colleges and universities and online, and has written an invited article, "Clickers: A Classroom Innovation," that appeared in the October 2007 issue of *National Education Association Advocate*. His clickers Web site, www.vanderbilt.edu/cft/crs.htm, featuring a bibliography with over 170 entries, receives almost two thousand visits a month.

His other research interests include the role of preclass reading assignments in mathematics courses, the role of teaching in the academic hiring process, and, in Bruff's home discipline of mathematics, adapting traditional wavelet methods to nonuniform settings.

CHAPTER ONE

ENGAGING STUDENTS WITH CLICKERS

Classroom response systems are instructional technologies that allow instructors to rapidly collect and analyze student responses to questions posed during class. Systems are typically used in the following manner. First, an instructor poses a question, often a multiple-choice question, to the students. The students think about the question and submit their responses to the questions using handheld wireless transmitters, usually called *clickers*, which often look like television remote controls, and beam signals to a receiving device attached to the instructor's classroom computer. Software on the computer produces a bar chart showing the distribution of student answers. Instructors then use these results to decide how to proceed during class: having students engage in small-group or classwide discussions on the question at hand, moving on to the next topic if the results indicate students are ready, or something else entirely.

For example, I once displayed the question in Example 1.1 in a course on probability. After giving students a minute or two to think about and respond to the question without discussing it with each other, I had my classroom response system generate the bar chart shown in Figure 1.1 as a summary of the student responses. Since the correct answer to the question is "one boy and one girl," an answer that only four of the sixteen students selected, I then had the students discuss the question in pairs. After a minute or two of lively discussion, the students voted again using their clickers. The system then produced the bar chart shown in Figure 1.2, indicating to me that the small-group discussion time was productive and that most students had a better understanding of the question.

I then asked for a student who changed his or her mind from "all are equally likely" to "one boy and one girl" to share with the class the reasons for doing so. One of my students volunteered and offered an explanation of the question. I listened to the explanation and responded by drawing an appropriate diagram on the chalkboard, offering a supplemental explanation, and then asking for student questions. In less than ten minutes, most students came to their own understanding of the question at hand.

Example 1.1

Your sister-in-law calls to say that she's having twins. Which of the following is more likely? (Assume that she's not having identical twins.)

A. Twin boys

B. Twin girls

C. One boy and one girl

D. All are equally likely

Derek Bruff, Mathematics, Vanderbilt University

The use of small-group discussion in the manner described is usually called *peer instruction*, after Mazur (1997), and is described in more detail later in this chapter. The choice of the instructor

FIGURE 1.1. SAMPLE RESULTS FROM FIRST VOTE.

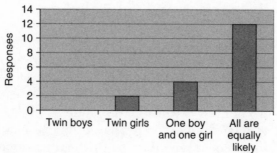

FIGURE 1.2. SAMPLE RESULTS FROM SECOND VOTE.

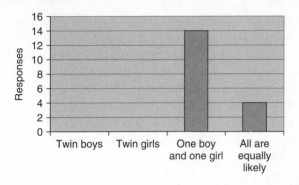

to have students engage in peer instruction after seeing the results of the first vote is an example of what is sometimes called *agile teaching* (Beatty, Gerace, Leonard, & Dufresne, 2006), an approach to using classroom response systems explored in Chapter Two. The question in Example 1.1 might be classified as an application question since it requires students to apply the notion of a probability space to a particular situation. The example question, activity, and results described are drawn from my own teaching, but many other instructors use similar questions and similar techniques in their own disciplines. As the remainder of this book makes clear, however, there are many ways to use clickers in the classroom.

Since classroom response systems rely on students' submitting their responses to questions with handheld clickers, using these systems requires some way of distributing clickers to students. At some institutions, students purchase clickers sold at the campus bookstores, right alongside textbooks and graphing calculators. A clicker usually costs between twenty and sixty dollars. Some textbook publishers bundle reduced-cost clickers with their textbooks. At these institutions, students bring their clickers with them to class and use them in multiple courses. Instructors often have students register their clickers to allow instructors to track and sometimes grade individual student responses. For example, students might enter their clicker serial numbers in their local online course management system, allowing instructors to import those serial numbers along with student names to their classroom response system software. After each class session in which clickers are used, instructors can assign participation grades to the students in the class based on their responses to questions.

On other campuses, schools or departments purchase sets of clickers for instructors to use. An instructor brings a box of clickers to class, and students pick one up on their way into the room. They use the clickers during class to respond to questions and return them to the box on their way out of the classroom. This method of distribution makes it easy for students to use clickers anonymously. If instructors using this method are interested in tracking student responses, the clickers might be clearly labeled with numbers and students instructed to pick up the same clickers in each class session. A spreadsheet that matches student names with clicker numbers can then be used to track and grade individual responses.

Instructors using classroom response systems also require receivers and appropriate software. Some instructors borrow receivers from instructional technology or classroom media offices or their departments. Other instructors use free or reduced-cost receivers from vendors or textbook publishers. The software for these systems is usually available for free download from vendor Web sites. Many vendors' software programs include gradebook tools allowing instructors to track and manage student clicker grades and export them to commonly used online course management systems. Getting started using response systems can take some instructors some time. Chapter Five provides more on this issue, as well as information on the technical and logistical features of various systems.

Classroom response system technology dates back at least to the 1960s. Early systems used transmitters and receivers connected by wires instead of the infrared and radio frequency wireless connections of today's systems. Many of the ways today's systems are used to engage and assess students were described in the literature on these early systems. (Judson and Sawada, 2002, provide a review of this literature, as well as some historical information on early systems. Historical information is also provided in Abrahamson, 2006, and Judson and Sawada, 2006.)

Classroom response systems are known by many other names, including *student response systems, audience response systems, personal response systems, classroom communication systems, group response systems*, and *electronic voting systems*, and others too. I use *classroom response system* in this book as a popular and fitting term for these systems. *Audience response system* is another popular term (Banks, 2006), but some instructors who use clickers to engage students during class dislike the idea of describing students as audience members given the passive role audiences usually play in other settings. *Student response system* is also a useful term, but it can be used to describe online as well as classroom response systems. This book focuses on the use of these kinds of systems in face-to-face classrooms, although some of the principles and strategies for using classroom systems are likely to apply in online settings.

Some instructors interested in teaching with classroom response systems are curious to know what research studying their effectiveness has been conducted. The consensus of several literature reviews (Caldwell, 2007; Fies & Marshall, 2006; Judson & Sawada, 2002; Roschelle, Penuel, & Abrahamson, 2004; Simpson & Oliver, 2007) seems to be that the use of clickers often increases student attendance, participation, and enjoyment of classes and provides students and instructors with useful feedback on student learning. Most students and instructors like using clickers, which they find fun and enjoyable to use. There also seems to be consensus regarding the impact of classroom response systems on student learning. The impact depends in large measure on the instructional methods by which clickers are used. Teaching methods that use active learning, such as small-group and classwide discussion methods, typically result in improved student learning over methods in which students play more passive roles. It is not clear from the literature the extent to which classroom response system technology plays a role in these learning gains. It is possible that the methods themselves are responsible for learning gains, and clicker technology merely facilitates and supports those methods. This finding motivates much of the discussion of teaching choices found in this book since it appears that how instructors choose to use classroom response systems is the most important variable in their impact on student learning. Most literature reviews call for further research into the effects of clickers on student learning. I hope that this book, particularly the reasons for using clickers outlined in Chapter Six, will provide future researchers with useful frameworks for their investigations.

One reason to use classroom response systems is that they have the ability to allow every student to respond to a question and the ability to display the distribution of student responses for all students to see. These abilities can make a classroom response system an effective tool for engaging students during class. Here the term *engagement* refers to more than just participation in class. Engaged students are those who are actively involved in class discussions and thinking intentionally about course content during class. Classroom response systems can be used to engage students in a variety of ways, including classwide and small-group discussions, that can foster active learning in the classroom.

GENERATING CLASSWIDE DISCUSSIONS

One common use of classroom response systems is generating and fostering classwide discussion. A typical structure for doing so might be called "think-vote-share," after the "think-pair-share" classroom engagement technique first proposed by Lyman (1981), which many instructors use without clickers. Instructors using clickers in this way first pose a multiple-choice question to their students. Students think about the question and submit their answers using their clickers. The instructor then displays the bar chart generated by the system showing the results of the question, indicating how many students selected each answer choice. These results, along with the thinking that students do prior to submitting their responses, inform and enhance subsequent classwide discussion facilitated by the instructor.

Case Study: Communication Studies

Michael Dorsher teaches a course on mass media ethics at the University of Wisconsin at Eau Claire. Each section of the course has between thirty and forty students. In the past, section sizes tended to be smaller, and the sections were oriented toward discussion. As enrollment in the course grew, Dorsher found it more difficult to have the kinds of discussions in which he wanted his students to engage. He now uses a classroom response system to help generate these kinds of discussions. For example, he presents his students with the following ethical dilemma: Suppose you are an editor at the *Washington Post*, and the Unabomber has demanded that you print his thirty-thousand-word manifesto or he will continue sending mail bombs as acts of terrorism. Dorsher then poses the first two questions in Example 1.2, asking his students to identify the values and loyalties that would be most important to them in this situation and leading a classwide discussion after each question. He then poses the third question in Example 1.2, asking them to identify the ethical philosophy and course of action that best matches the most important value and loyalty identified in the previous two questions.

Example 1.2

Question 1. As *Post* editor, which would you value most?

A. Upholding First Amendment independence from government

B. Increased readership

C. Maintaining credibility

D. Possibly helping save lives

E. Informing readers

F. Not acquiescing to terrorists

G. Possibly helping capture a criminal

Question 2. As *Post* editor, to whom do you most owe loyalty?

A. The terrorist, who's threatening you

B. Future potential victims of the terrorist

C. The surviving victims and families of dead victims

D. The government

E. Your readers/the public

F. Yourself and other journalists

Question 3. With a top value of _____ and a top loyalty of _____, which ethicist would you follow?

A. John Rawls: Protect the vulnerable; print the manifesto.

B. John Stuart Mill: The greatest good for the greatest number; don't print it to uphold press independence.

C. Aristotle: The golden mean would be to excerpt it in the paper and publish it all online.

Michael Dorsher, Communication and Journalism, University of Wisconsin at Eau Claire

Dorsher's third question can be particularly challenging for students since it may not have a single right answer depending on the value and loyalty selections the students chose in the first two questions. Students are required to select the one answer they feel best matches the responses to the earlier questions. On a quiz or exam, this kind of ambiguity would be a problem in a multiple-choice question. However, for a question used to foster in-class discussion, this ambiguity is a strength: it creates the opportunity for students to share and discuss the reasons they have for selecting particular answer choices, thereby encouraging critical thinking.

Dorsher finds that without clickers, often the vocal minority of students in his class ends up making the decisions on the first two questions. With clickers, more student voices are heard, and the majority makes the decision instead. One danger he finds in this process is that sometimes the minority can be silenced by the fact that they know they are in the minority, a fact made evident by the display of the clicker results to the entire class. Dorsher is careful to encourage the minority to express and defend their reasoning, playing the role of devil's advocate as necessary to keep the discussion going.

WHY USE CLICKERS FOR CLASSWIDE DISCUSSIONS?

Although classwide discussion is a frequently used instructional technique, it is worth mentioning a few reasons to have students engage in these discussions. Since students are often better able to make sense of ideas and concepts when they are given the chance to process those ideas and concepts in some way as they are learning about them, classwide discussion can be a useful way to help students learn during class. A lively classwide discussion can also help students pay attention and stay engaged during class. Classwide discussions also help instructors leverage the social aspects of the community of learners that constitutes a classroom. For instance, students often appreciate the chance to hear from and get to know each other, a process that can occur during a classwide discussion. Furthermore, sometimes students are better able to follow an explanation given by a peer than one given by their instructor. Classwide discussions provide opportunities for students to hear each other describe and grapple with course content.

Classroom response systems can augment classwide discussions in several ways. For example, instructors not using clickers often pose a question to their students, then ask for student volunteers to share their answers to the question. This approach has the disadvantage that students who do not volunteer answers need not engage seriously with the question. Some do, of course, but some may not, preferring to wait and hear from their peers before thinking deeply about the question at hand. Since students are more likely to learn when they do their own thinking, it is useful to encourage as many to think independently about a question as possible. Clickers can help make that happen since each student is asked to respond to a question before hearing other students' answers. This gives all students a chance to thoughtfully respond to a question, setting the stage for a productive class discussion that involves more students who are ready to share their diverse thoughts and perspectives.

Clickers give all students the chance to respond to a question independently, including shy students who might be hesitant to speak up in front of their peers, students who take more time to compose responses than might be provided otherwise, and students who simply would not be heard due to time constraints. This gives more students a voice in the classroom, as Dorsher observes, and helps these students prepare to participate more fully in a class discussion.

Since clickers allow students to respond to a question without their peers knowing their answers, they provide students with a level of anonymity that can encourage participation. Students who might not voice their opinions about a topic publicly for fear of being in the minority are given a chance to register those opinions with their clickers. When responding to questions with right and wrong answers, some students are hesitant to volunteer their responses publicly out of fear of being wrong in front of their peers. Clickers allow these students to answer questions honestly and risk being wrong.

Furthermore, although students cannot use a classroom response system to identify the individual responses of their peers, instructors may do so after class. This allows instructors to hold students accountable for their participation in a class session. It can remove the students' "cloaks of invisibility," a phrase used by Lee Shulman (quoted in Merrow, 2007) to describe the anonymity that students can use to avoid participation and engagement. Each student's responses to clicker questions can be viewed by instructors after class and factored into participation or other course grades. Knowing the system has this capability, students are often more likely to participate constructively in class.

The results of a clicker question can be displayed for an entire class to see, and this feature can help encourage discussion as well. For instance, students can learn that some classmates have different ideas and opinions, encouraging some students to want to hear more from those with different views. Also, students can learn that they are not alone in their ideas and opinions, which can encourage them to voice their thoughts during a discussion. This feature of classroom response systems can be a challenge as well, as Dorsher noted. Sometimes students who find themselves unexpectedly in the minority can be less eager to participate in a classwide discussion. Instructors often need to be careful when facilitating discussions in these situations. In addition, the display of clicker question results can demonstrate to students who answer a question correctly that many of their peers do not understand the question as well as they do. This can help justify to these students the use of class time devoted to exploring the question further.

Case Study: Biological Sciences

Adam Rich teaches a sophomore-level course in anatomy and physiology at the State University of New York College at Brockport that typically enrolls about 170 students. He uses clicker questions to generate classwide discussions that focus on the reasons for right and wrong answers to those questions in an effort to help students learn to build arguments.

Rather than using the think-vote-share activity, Rich poses a question to his students and has them submit their initial answers using their clickers. Instead of displaying the results to the students, he facilitates a classwide discussion of the question while allowing students to change their answers at any time. The classroom response system Rich uses allows him to monitor the distribution of responses as they change, providing him with information about how students are changing their minds during the discussion. He can use this information to continue the discussion until the students converge on the correct answer. Since the students cannot see the distribution of responses as they are submitted, they tend not to change their minds out of any kind of peer pressure. Instead, Rich finds that they consider and respond to the arguments their peers make during the discussion.

Rich has occasionally left the bar chart showing the real-time distribution of responses on the classroom projector screen for the students to see. When he did this, there was almost immediate convergence to a single answer choice, demonstrating what can happen when students do not respond independently to a classroom question. Instead of making sense of the arguments their peers put forth in favor of various answer choices, many students simply changed their responses to the most popular response, likely assuming that the popular answer was the correct one. Rich's clicker questions count toward 5 percent of his students' course grades. By not showing students the current responses to a clicker question but allowing them to change their responses during the discussion, he uses his students' interest in performing well in the course to motivate them to engage productively in his classwide discussions. He finds that students do so as long as they have the chance to change their answer choice to the correct one.

Case Study: Language Instruction

Karina Kline-Gabel teaches intermediate- and upper-level Spanish courses at James Madison University in Virginia, many of which have around forty-five students. She uses clickers frequently for oral exercises in her classes. For example, she might display a piece of artwork on her classroom projector screen and make a series of statements about the artwork. She asks her students to use their clickers to label each statement as correct or incorrect based on the grammar and vocabulary used in the statement. Often she makes the first few statements rather comically incorrect, probing students' vocabulary, before moving on to more challenging grammar issues. Clicker questions focused on grammar and vocabulary function to warm up students for more complex, subsequent tasks, such as discussing their opinions of the artwork.

Many of Kline-Gabel's clicker questions are correct-incorrect or true-false questions. Although students are likely to guess at correct answers to these questions half the time, Kline-Gabel almost always follows such a question with another question that asks students for reasons for their answers. For instance, she might ask, "The sentence was not correct. What was the mistake in the sentence?" and provide students with several possible choices. Kline-Gabel also often leads a classwide discussion of the correct-incorrect or true-false question that elicits reasons for student answers. Since her students know that they will be asked to supply reasons for their responses, she finds that they tend to take the questions seriously and not guess randomly. Her clicker questions, then, function to have students commit to answers to questions before a classwide discussion. This commitment can help them engage more actively in that discussion since they have a more vested interested in defending their answer choices.

Kline-Gabel finds that these exercises help students improve their second-language listening skills, in part because they isolate those skills from reading, writing, and speaking skills. She often conducts clicker-enhanced listening activities in lieu of activities in which students work independently on reading and writing activities. She finds that her students ask more questions about a clicker question they miss than they will about a reading exercise they do not understand. She believes this is because the clicker questions are discussed as a class, whereas a student with a question about a reading exercise has to raise his or her hand to ask it. Discussing difficulties as a class somehow makes it more acceptable for students to ask questions. Furthermore, she finds that when students are engaged in individual work in or out of class, they often move too quickly through that work, not engaging in it as seriously as they could. Clicker questions allow her to slow down

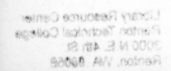

her students' pace, encouraging them to engage in the work more seriously and ask more questions. She also finds that her clicker activities help her students stay on task more than small-group activities.

STRATEGIES FOR LEADING CLASSWIDE DISCUSSIONS

Many instructors have experience effectively leading classwide discussions. However, since classroom response systems provide each student in a class the opportunity to think about and respond to a discussion question and display a bar chart showing the distribution of student responses to the instructor and often the entire class, leading a discussion after a clicker question is a somewhat different task from other kinds of discussion leading. Following are some strategies for leading a classwide discussion following a clicker question.

1. *Have students share the reasoning behind their answers to the clicker question.* For many questions, those reasons are more important for students to understand than a particular answer. Also, students are sometimes able to understand their peers' explanations more quickly than those offered by their instructors.
2. *Make sure to hear from students about each of the more popular answer choices.* Some classroom response systems allow instructors to see how each student responded to a question, allowing those instructors to call on students who chose particular answers. More typically, however, instructors might say something like, "Can I hear from a student who chose answer A?"
3. *If no student volunteers to defend or explain a particular answer choice, instructors might step in and suggest some reasons for that choice.* They might also ask students to hypothesize why someone might find that choice reasonable. Since it is often useful for students to think through wrong answers as well as right ones, spending some time on wrong or unpopular answers can be important.
4. *Encourage students to respond to and challenge each other's comments during the discussion.* A discussion in which students reason

with and debate each other can often lead to deeper learning than one in which the instructor does all the challenging and debating.

5. *Refrain from making important points during the discussion if those points can be made by the students.* The understanding that students gain by discovering the points themselves is often longer lasting. If students miss a few key points in their discussion, an instructor can always make them at the end of the discussion.

6. *Sometimes students have trouble hearing each other's comments during a classwide discussion.* Instructors who observe this should repeat student comments loudly enough for the entire class to hear.

7. *Do not reveal the correct answer to a clicker question, if there is one, too soon.* This can stifle discussion. (See Chapter Four for more on this choice.)

Beatty, Leonard, Gerace, and Dufresne (2006) elaborate on some of these strategies and provide additional ones. Their focus is on teaching science with classroom response systems, but their advice for leading clicker-based discussions should be useful to instructors in many disciplines.

Generating Small-Group Discussions

Perhaps the most common method of engaging students in the learning process with a classroom response system is the use of peer instruction (PI), a method popularized by Harvard University physics professor Eric Mazur in his book *Peer Instruction: A User's Manual* (1997). Most instructors implement PI by first posing a multiple-choice question. Students think about the question silently and independently and submit their answers with their clickers. The instructor then displays a bar chart showing the results. Instead of moving to a classwide discussion at this point, the next step in PI is to have the students discuss the question in pairs or small groups. This is the essential feature of PI: having students share and discuss their answers with each other in small groups. Each student helps instruct his or her peers. After this discussion time, students again answer the same clicker question, this time submitting answers informed by their small-group discussions.

Often the results of the second vote are different from those of the first, and for questions with correct answers, often there is some convergence to the correct answer in the students' responses.

Case Study: Physics

Steven Pollock uses PI to engage students in the physics courses he teaches at the University of Colorado at Boulder. After the vote that follows the PI time, if the students are split among more than one answer choice, he usually asks for volunteers to share reasons for their answers. Occasionally he polls his students again after this brief classwide discussion. He usually allocates two or three minutes for PI and typically asks four to six PI clicker questions during a fifty-minute lecture.

Most of the questions Pollock uses with PI are conceptual in nature, after the ones Mazur (1997) describes. (See Example 3.3 for a sample conceptual question that Pollock uses.) He also likes to ask application questions to help students extend concepts to new contexts. For instance, he might ask students, "How many controls in your car are designed to modify your acceleration?" He and his physics department colleagues have developed question banks for many undergraduate physics courses and made them available online (Pollock, n.d.).

Some of Pollock's colleagues in the physics department have undergraduate teaching assistants who circulate among students during PI time, answering questions and prompting students to think more deeply about the questions. They have large enough teaching staffs and ask enough clicker questions so that each small group of students interacts with at least one member of the teaching staff during each class period.

Pollock finds that physics students, particularly those who are not science majors, expect physics to be about solving computational problems correctly. Pollock believes that physics is more often about conceptual understanding and scientific reasoning, not exclusively computation. Thus, the small-group and classwide discussions of reasons behind answers to clicker questions, particularly those that are conceptual or applied in nature, are the most important parts of class from Pollock's point of view. Students, however, do not always see the value in these discussions given their understanding of the discipline of physics, at least not initially.

WHY USE CLICKERS FOR SMALL-GROUP DISCUSSIONS?

There are a number of reasons that having students engage in small-group discussions during class can enhance their learning experience. Perhaps the most important of these reasons is that asking students to discuss a given question with their peers is a way of actively engaging them in course material. When students are actively making sense of course material, they tend to learn the material more deeply and more quickly. Small-group discussions allow more students to participate actively than is possible in classwide discussions.

Another reason was expressed by Anthony Crider, who teaches astronomy at Elon University. He believes that if he had an infinite amount of time, he could talk to each of his students individually about a given question, assessing the student's understanding, diagnosing the student's misconceptions, and responding in ways tailored to that student's particular learning needs. Because he does not have an infinite amount of time, he uses PI to encourage this process to happen between students. Student-to-student instruction is perhaps not as effective as instructor-to-student instruction, but it can be very useful and practical, particularly in large courses.

Small-group discussions, such as those used in PI, also help prepare students to participate more fully in subsequent classwide discussions because students have the opportunity to develop and test their ideas before being asked to share them with the entire class. There can be strength in numbers too. It is one thing to speak up in class and say, "I think the answer is . . ." It is another thing to speak up and say, "*We* think the answer is . . ." Small-group discussions can encourage students to voice their thoughts during a classwide discussion since students can develop allies in other students who agree with them.

A classroom response system can foster these positive effects of small-group discussion. Having students respond individually and independently to a clicker question before engaging in PI time can improve the quality of that time since doing so gives students a chance to develop some thoughts to bring to the small-group discussion. This can be particularly important for shy students and other students who might not otherwise participate in a discussion, even one conducted in a small group. Since classroom response systems allow instructors to track student responses, having students respond to a clicker question before or after a small-group discussion creates some accountability that can encourage students to engage more seriously in that discussion. Some instructors require students in a small group to agree on a common answer to a clicker question before submitting their responses. This forces students to work toward consensus and can focus and energize small-group discussions and help prepare students for other life experiences in which building consensus is important. Furthermore, since a classroom response system can display the results of pre- and postdiscussion clicker questions, any convergence or divergence in student viewpoints caused by the small-group discussions is made visible to the students. This can show students that small-group discussions have an impact on their learning.

A variety of studies have been conducted investigating the effects of PI on student learning. Crouch and Mazur (2001) share data from ten years of teaching physics with PI at Harvard University, and Fagen, Crouch, and Mazur (2002) report results from eleven higher education institutions. Both reports argue for PI's positive effects on student learning. (See the literature reviews mentioned earlier in the chapter for other studies.)

Case Study: Language Instruction

Parvanak Fassihi uses clickers in the course on academic writing for international students she teaches at Boston University. Her students speak a variety of first languages and are learning to write in a second language, English. Most classes have around fifteen students. As a second-language course, the focus of the course tends to be on grammar and sentence-level writing issues.

Fassihi uses clickers to generate small-group discussions. A typical lesson might be on run-on sentences. She starts by giving a brief lecture on the topic. Then she has her students identify and fix run-on sentences listed on a worksheet in groups of three or four. She then reviews the sentences with the entire class by asking her students to respond to the question, "Is this a run-on sentence? Yes or no," for each sentence. The students respond individually using their clickers, and Fassihi displays the results.

If the results are mixed, she has the students return to their groups to discuss the sentence again, then leads a class discussion about the sentence.

Since Fassihi finds that only 5 to 10 percent of her students volunteer to speak up during class at the start of a semester, she feels she needs groups of three or four students to encourage group discussion. If she were to pair students, she would likely have several pairs of shy students who would not talk within their pairs. With slightly larger groups, there is a greater chance that each group will have at least one student willing to talk.

Each of Fassihi's students responds individually to each question, but each group receives points equal to the number of correct answers submitted by members of that group. This encourages the students to try to convince each other of the correct answer during the group discussion time. Each group's score is tallied by the classroom response system Fassihi uses, and at the end of class, she presents the scores. These scores are not factored into the students' course grades, but they add an element of friendly competition to class. Fassihi often has some kind of prize, usually chocolate, for the winning group.

Fassihi finds the PI element of her lessons to be an effective way to encourage interaction among her students and with her. This is often a difficult goal to achieve in second-language courses. Also, since the students see that they have a voice in the course with their clickers, they are encouraged to have a literal voice in the course as well.

Case Study: Veterinary Medicine

Holly Bender teaches a 110-student course in veterinary pathology at Iowa State University. The course features a large number of case studies designed to teach students to interpret laboratory data. Her approach to teaching this course is based on the work of Larry Michaelsen, a proponent of team-based learning (Michaelsen, Knight, & Fink, 2004). She uses a three-class sequence for most topics. On the first day, she lectures about the topic, asking clicker questions along the way to help students engage in the lecture. Then her students complete two complex case studies on the topic as homework prior to the next class period. On the second day, she presents her students with a third case, similar to one of the two assigned as homework. The students answer a series of multiple-choice questions about the case, first as individuals and then as teams. She uses the team responses to lead a classwide discussion of the case. On the third day, she provides the students with a fourth case, this one featuring several erroneous claims that are not supported sufficiently by the case study data. The students have to identify these claims, first as individuals and then as teams.

Given the technological limitations of the classroom response system that Bender initially used, she gave each team a single clicker, forcing her students to decide on a common team answer. The system she uses now does not force any limitation on the number of clickers in use at any one time. However, she still gives each team a single clicker since she finds the resulting class dynamic highly effective. As a result, her students answer the quiz questions on class days 2 and 3 individually using answer sheets and as teams using clickers.

Bender finds that her students are initially overwhelmed by this course structure since it is so different from the ones to which they are accustomed, but by the start of the last third of the semester, her students have learned how to work effectively within this structure. In fact, by that point in the semester, it is rare that a team answers a question incorrectly since the students develop such effective working relationships within their teams.

For the class sessions focused on case studies, Bender has students read and analyze a case study and respond to multiple-choice questions about the case study first as individuals. When all the team members complete their quizzes, a team representative brings their answer sheets to the front of the room. Once the first team does so, Bender gives the other teams five minutes to complete their individual quizzes. After those five minutes, the team members discuss the questions among themselves. Once the first team has arrived at its collective response, Bender gives the remaining teams five minutes to conclude. Then she has the teams respond to the questions using the clickers. After each vote, she selects a team at random to explain its answer, which initiates a classwide discussion on the question, sometimes resulting in vigorous debates among teams. By the end of the class, she attempts to make the reasoning behind the correct answers to the questions clear.

The six-member teams Bender uses last throughout the semester and are designed to be as heterogeneous as possible, particularly in terms of small- or large-animal specializations. Half of a student's grade in her course is determined by the in-class quizzes. Each team decides how to apportion that grade among three components: the individual quiz responses, the team quiz responses, and an online peer assessment each team member completes. Most teams choose to weigh the team responses more than the other two components, since they know they are more likely to be correct as a team. However, they also want individual accountability, so they usually allocate at least 15 percent of their quiz grades to each of the other two components.

Bender recognizes that team dynamics can sometimes cause problems. For instance, some teams often have an overly assertive team member, one who discourages or ignores the sharing of multiple perspectives during team discussions. However, Bender finds that if that team member answers incorrectly a few times, then the other team members start to ignore that member's assertiveness. As a result, many team-dynamic problems are self-correcting. Her students are older and typically more self-motivated than undergraduate students. They are also very competitive and put pressure on themselves to achieve. Bender finds her team-based learning process works in spite of that, and it helps to teach the students the cooperation and communication skills that employers often identify as important.

The advantages of the team-based learning structure outweigh any problems in Bender's opinion. For instance, she has seen students vigorously debating sodium balance, a very dry topic, after class. Bender sees her role in this process as setting up the right cases and questions for students to answer, providing feedback along the way, and letting students learn.

FREQUENTLY ASKED QUESTIONS ABOUT PEER INSTRUCTION

Should students respond to a clicker question individually before engaging in PI?

There are advantages in having students answer a question individually before discussing it with their peers. Some instructors consider this step an essential component of the PI process since it encourages students to think independently and provides students a chance to formulate a few thoughts they can bring to the PI time, creating the possibility of more productive small-group discussions. For example, Anthony Crider, who teaches astronomy at Elon University, has his students respond to a few questions designed to surface their misconceptions about the phases of the moon and the causes of the seasons at the beginning of units on those two topics. He feels that having students respond to these clicker questions motivates them to commit to their ideas on these two topics, preparing them to participate more fully in subsequent small-group discussions.

The results of a first, individual set of responses can also affect the pace of the class. If a large majority of students answer a question correctly on the first try, an instructor might choose to skip the PI time entirely, saving some class time. For this reason, some instructors find it particularly useful to have students respond individually to questions they suspect students will find relatively easy. For similar reasons, when asking a question instructors suspect students will find very difficult, they might skip the individual vote and proceed directly to the PI time.

Ivan Shibley teaches chemistry at Penn State Berks, and he usually does not have his students think about and respond to his clicker questions individually prior to PI time. He chooses not to do so in part because of limited class time, but more because he feels that his chemistry students often do not have preconceived ideas about questions and topics in his course. As a result, he finds his students often need PI time in order to get started answering a question. Matthew Mulvaney, who teaches statistics courses for psychology students at the State University of University at Brockport, often skips the individual response phase of the standard PI process as well. He does so because the course material is challenging and students often need group work time to get any traction on the questions he asks given the constraints of class time. There is also some evidence (Len, 2007) that students who self-identify as not particularly skilled in math and science prefer to collaborate when answering clicker questions when given the chance.

If students are fairly enthusiastic about discussing course content or a particular topic during class, instructors may find that they welcome the chance to jump right into small-group discussions. Kristen Hessler teaches philosophy at the State University of New York at Albany. She allows her students to confer with each other prior to answering clicker questions if they so choose. Some students take advantage of this opportunity and work regularly in the same small groups to answer questions. These students find PI an energizing component of class.

Under what conditions should instructors skip PI after students respond individually?

If a clicker question has a single correct answer and that answer is clearly the most popular one, an instructor might choose to move on to the next question or topic without having students engage in PI since these results likely indicate a high level of understanding among the students of the question at hand. However, sometimes students answer a question correctly without having thought deeply about their responses. If an instructor suspects that to be the case, then PI time may be appropriate. It is important to note that if an instructor shows students results such as these, students are likely to assume that the popular answer is the correct answer, which can reduce their participation in PI time. (See Chapter Four for a discussion of the choice to show students the results of a clicker question.)

If a clicker question has a single correct answer but one of the incorrect answers is clearly the most popular one, then the question is likely one that the students find challenging, and engaging the students in PI is likely to be productive. Sometimes two students with wrong answers will help each other discover the correct answer (particularly if they have different wrong answers and can make arguments against each of their original answer choices), so PI time can be fruitful in this case. However, instructors might find that even more students are convinced of the popular wrong answer after PI time, particularly when instructors show them the results of the initial vote, results that could lead students to believe that the popular answer is the correct one. (See Chapter Two for suggestions for handling this kind of situation.)

If two or more of the answer choices turn out to be popular among students' individual responses, then the stage is set for productive PI time. Each small group of students is likely to contain students with different perspectives on the question at hand, so the small-group discussion is likely to be lively and productive. Many instructors strive to write clicker questions that produce results of this sort not only because they lead to more engaging PI, but also because split decisions like these imply that the question is of an appropriate difficulty level for students—not so challenging that very few of them can answer it correctly, but not so easy that most of them answer it correctly. Showing students the results of the initial vote in this case is often helpful in encouraging discussion since the mixed results of the vote let students know that the question is one worth addressing.

See Chapter Two for further discussion of responding to the results of clicker questions.

What instructions should students be given for PI time?

Instructors can instruct students how to form pairs or small groups in different ways. An instructor might say, "Pair up with a student nearby," or give a more specific instruction: "Find a student nearby who answered differently from you." The latter option requires a little more time and student effort, but if students are split among more than one answer choice, more productive small-group discussions may ensue. Bill Hill, who teaches psychology at Kennesaw State University, often uses the latter instruction, particularly when the results of the individual responses to a clicker question are mixed. He points out that when students follow this instruction, at least one student in each pair of students is incorrect, setting the stage for more productive PI time. He often sees convergence to correct answers on the post-PI set of responses to his clicker questions.

Instructors can also specify the task in which the pairs or small groups should engage. An instructor might say, "Share the reasons you have for your answer with your partners," or, "Convince your partners that you have the correct answer." The latter option assumes that the question at hand has a correct answer, of course, and it fosters a somewhat more competitive class atmosphere than the former option, which may or may not align well with the goals of some instructors, but it also provides focus for PI time. Given that some students might be discussing the question with other students who answered similarly, instructors might add, "If you and your partner agree on the answer to the question, go ahead and explain your reasons since both of you may be wrong."

Instructors might also say, "Come to a consensus with your partners on an answer choice." This provides more focus to the small-group discussion time and a framework for more engaged discussions. Building consensus often takes some time, however, so this instruction has an impact on the pace of the class. Instructors need not actually require consensus answers from each group as Holly Bender does in her team-based learning courses. Instead, they can instruct students to attempt to gain consensus but answer individually after the PI time.

Adam Lucas, who teaches mathematics at Saint Mary's College of California, is interested in the effects of seating arrangements, group dynamics, and classroom management choices on student participation and learning, particularly the role of what he calls "high-status" students—those who are perceived by their peers as doing well in the course—in dominating small-group and classwide discussion (Lucas, 2007). He often monitors student discussions in class and moves students who are not working well together. He finds that social dynamics can be a serious issue and that he needs to be proactive with seating arrangements and instructions for class discussions. The first time he used clickers, he says class was a bit of a "free-for-all." By interviewing his students about their experiences in his class, he learned they needed more structure. One approach he uses is to say, "Even if the two of you agree on your answer, go through the steps and check your work." This works better, in his opinion, than the "convince your neighbor that you're correct" approach.

Should each small group submit a single response following PI time?

Holly Bender of Iowa State University has her students work in small groups during class to answer clicker questions, and each group is required to submit a common group response to these questions. This gives each group a specific goal for their discussion time that can help students focus their attention and energy. Students who must come to a consensus often have more motivation to engage in the critical thinking necessary to analyze each other's arguments and defend their own arguments. Not requiring consensus makes it a little easier for students to step back from this process and not try to integrate their perspectives with those of their peers. Also, in their future professional and personal interactions, students frequently have to come to consensus with friends and colleagues. Structuring PI time in this way provides practice for students in consensus-building skills. Furthermore, students are more likely to speak up during subsequent classwide discussion if they know that they have the support of their fellow group members in their answer choices, and they are also more likely to be interested in hearing an instructor's explanation of a question if they and their group have come to consensus around an incorrect answer. Building consensus takes time, however. Peer instruction that leads to a single response per group is likely to take more class time than PI without single responses per group. This class time, of course, could be time well spent.

Instructors who grade group responses on accuracy provide additional motivation for students to engage seriously in group discussion and consensus building. But graded group responses can also lead to some unproductive social dynamics within groups. Edna Ross teaches psychology at the University of Louisville and is cautious about the use of graded group responses. She has known minority students to take issue with the use of graded group assignments in other courses. They find that sometimes majority students ignore or minimize the input of minority students when grades are on the line. This can happen for a variety of reasons, some of which can be related to the student's status as a minority in the classroom. The minority student can experience fairly intense pressure to answer a question correctly every single time as a way to prove his or her "worth" to the group. As Holly Bender points out, the issue of students who dominate the group decision-making process and are wrong can often correct itself rather quickly. It would seem that difficulties can arise when a student dominates the group and answers questions correctly. This can lead to problematic group dynamics and likely calls for the kinds of intervention Adam Lucas uses in his mathematics courses.

What should instructors do during PI time?

Many instructors find it useful to circulate among students as they discuss a clicker question during PI time. Instructors might do so in order to eavesdrop on student conversations to get a better sense of how students are answering the question and the reasons they are giving for their answers. This information can be helpful for preparing for subsequent classwide discussion of the question, since it provides insight into why students make certain answer choices. It also provides instructors with students on whom they can call during the classwide discussion to share reasons for their answers.

Instructors might also stop and interact with a group of students, asking questions of them in order to prompt them to consider issues and cases not already discussed in the group. Simply providing them with hints or answers is not likely to be as useful as asking them questions designed to help them think through the question more deeply themselves. This tactic can be particularly helpful with groups in which the students quickly agree on the answer to the question at hand. Instructors can play the devil's advocate role in helping them consider other answer choices.

Teaching assistants, when available, can be instructed to circulate among students too. It can be helpful to give assistants specific instructions for their role. In particular, teaching assistants, who typically have limited experience teaching, are often more likely simply to give answers as they interact with students instead of asking them questions designed to help them discover the answers on their own. They might need guidance from their supervisors on this issue.

Circulating among students is not always possible, however. The ability to do so largely depends on the students' seating arrangement in a classroom. If it is not possible to walk among and interact with students during PI time, instructors might stand at the front of the classroom and observe students to get a sense of how quickly they analyze the question at hand and submit their answers and a sense of how many of them are staying on topic in their small-group discussions. This is also a useful time for instructors to review the answer choices to the clicker question and plan a strategy for discussing them with students.

How might an instructor lead a classwide discussion following PI time?

The strategies for leading more general classwide discussions apply equally as well to classwide discussions that follow PI time. One difference is that in traditional peer instruction, students answer a question twice: once on their own and once following a small-group discussion. Instructors can use this structure to enhance a classwide discussion by asking, for instance, for a student who changed his or her answer during the PI time to share with the class the reasons for that change. Instructors might also ask for a student who did not change his or her answer to share with the class reasons why he or she did not find peers' arguments persuasive. Instructors might also ask to hear from a group about the arguments shared during the group discussion time that were most persuasive.

CREATING TIMES FOR TELLING

Many instructors use classroom response systems to prepare students for "times for telling," a term Schwartz and Bransford (1998) use to describe moments in a learning experience when students are ready and interested to learn from a lecture or reading. Instructors usually pose a question with an answer choice that students with a particular common misconception are likely to select. Students think about the question and submit their answers using their clickers. If the question has its intended effect, more students choose the misconception-based answer choice than any other answer choice. The instructor then reveals the correct answer to the student, often by demonstrating the answer's veracity in some way. The students are then surprised to find out that so many of them answered incorrectly, which leads them to want to hear the instructor's explanation of the question and its correct and incorrect answers.

Case Study: Chemistry

Dennis Jacobs uses clickers in the introductory chemistry courses he teaches at the University of Notre Dame. These are large courses, often with around 240 students per section. Many of the questions he uses are tied to classroom chemistry demonstrations, the kind often performed in the front of chemistry lecture halls to show students chemistry in action. His clicker questions ask student to predict the results of these demonstrations.

For example, he has shown his students that running a circuit through a beaker of pure water does not light an attached light bulb since pure water does not conduct electricity. He then replaced the water in the beaker with a weak acidic solution, 2 percent $CH_3CO_2H_{(aq)}$. This lit the light bulb dimly, demonstrating that the acidic solution was a poor conductor of electricity. He then posed the following clicker question to his students: "Predict how well pure $CH_3CO_2H_{(l)}$ will light the light bulb. Will the light bulb be bright, dim, or dark?" Many students erroneously selected "bright," not realizing that the conduction of electricity requires both water and acid molecules. He then had his students discuss the question in pairs and respond to the question again. This second time, the majority of students chose "dark," the correct answer. He then engaged the students in a classwide discussion of the question, giving students the chance to share their reasons for their answers with the class. Then he repeated the experiment with the pure acid, demonstrating students that the pure acid did not conduct electricity and the light bulb remained dark.

Jacobs finds that by the time his students respond to the question individually, discuss the question with their peers, respond to the question again, and participate in a classwide discussion, they really want to know how the experiment turns out. He uses the experiment to show why a particular answer is correct and, after the experiment, revisits the arguments students make during the discussion in the light of the results of the experiment. Jacobs feels that if he performed the experiment first, then had the students discuss it, many students would focus their efforts on memorizing his explanation of the experiment. The process he uses focuses their attention on thinking critically.

One limitation of this approach is that it relies on experiments Jacobs designs to surface student misconceptions. When possible, Jacobs gives his students the chance to design their own experiments to test hypotheses. For example, many students think that boiling water means converting water molecules into hydrogen and oxygen gases, not changing the phase of the water from liquid to gas. Jacobs might ask his students a clicker question in which they have to identify the components of water vapor. Many choose incorrectly, indicating that water vapor consists of hydrogen and oxygen gases. He then asks his students to suggest a way they might test their hypothesis. Inevitably some student suggests burning the water vapor. If it really consists of hydrogen gas, burning the vapor should result in an explosion. Jacobs then performs this experiment in front of the class, playing up the possibility of an explosion for dramatic effect. Nothing happens, of course, leading students to conclude that water vapor must still be H_2O. He then prompts them to determine if they could have ruled out the hydrogen hypothesis on the basis of their past experience. Usually some student realizes that the fact that many people boil water for tea or coffee on gas stoves rules out their hypothesis. This helps his students start connecting their real-world experiences to the course content.

WHY USE CLICKERS TO CREATE TIMES FOR TELLING?

Students' intrinsic interest in learning in a particular discipline or course can vary dramatically. When students answer a question incorrectly, however, they are often more likely to want to know the correct answer and to hear an explanation of the question than if that same explanation is offered prior to the question. Not only are students more likely to want to understand the question, but they are also more likely to make sense of the explanation of the question since they have had a chance to think about it on their own. Thus, having students attempt to answer a question on a particular topic can be an effective way to create a time for telling, that is, a moment when students are ready and able to understand an explanation about that topic. The learning experience is all the better if the question is one that many students answer incorrectly due to some important misconception they have. That sets the stage for them to engage in the difficult process of resolving that misconception.

A classroom response system can play several important roles in this process. Having each student respond to a clicker question designed to surface some particular student misconception engages all, not just some, students in a process that helps prepare them for a time for telling. Moreover, by having students respond independently to the question prior to any small-group or classwide discussion, each student has a chance to consider his or her own ideas about the question and make connections between the question and his or her own set of prior experiences and knowledge. Furthermore, instructors using clickers to ask these kinds of questions are asking students to commit to their answers. Although that commitment merely takes the form of pressing a button on a clicker, that act can help students become more engaged with the question. This means that they will be all the more surprised by the correct answer and all the readier to hear an explanation. Also, the results from a clicker question of this sort can show students just how common a particular misconception or misunderstanding is. Students are surprised to find out that so many of their peers answer a question correctly. Finding that out can further motivate students to listen to and understand an explanation of the correct answer.

Case Study: Psychology

Edna Ross teaches psychology at the University of Louisville. Her courses tend to be very large, enrolling as many as 350 students each. Ross often uses clicker questions to create times for telling. For example, she finds that her students usually have difficulty distinguishing between classical and instrumental conditioning. She once told her students to take a five-minute break in the middle of her seventy-five-minute class session. She told them that she would play relaxing music and display some calming images on the classroom projector screen to help them get the most out of their break. She then displayed images of the ocean and played the ominous theme from the movie *Jaws*. Her students' supposed break was really a setup for a clicker question asking whether the use of the *Jaws* theme in this instance was an example of classical or instrumental conditioning. She had the students respond to the question with their clickers; as she expected, most selected the incorrect answer: instrumental conditioning. At this point, she did not tell the students the correct answer. Instead, she let students who chose instrumental conditioning volunteer their reasons, followed by the students who chose classical conditioning. This led to a spirited debate between the two groups of students, in part because the majority assumed they were correct. She then revealed the correct answer, not through a classroom demonstration but by using the correct answer indicator provided by her classroom response system. (The bar on the results bar chart belonging to the correct answer turned green.) At that point, the class "went wild" in Ross's words.

Ross feels that this question was particularly effective because her students had read about the two types of conditioning in their textbook but had not yet fully understood them. This meant that those participating in the classwide discussion of the question were not just relying on their intuition; they were drawing on their partial understanding of the preclass reading. Once Ross explained the correct answer to the students, she could see that they began to complete that partial understanding.

Ross finds that the act of clicking an answer choice is a way of committing to that answer, which hooks the students into the learning process. No commitment means no potential for change in understanding.

Strategies for Creating Times for Telling

Creating moments in a class session when students are ready to get the most out of a lecture or an explanation takes a certain set of circumstances. The strategies provided next can help instructors create conditions favorable for times for telling:

1. *Design questions that trap students around common misconceptions and ideas that are intuitive but not accurate.* This requires knowing what those common misconceptions and intuitions are. Instructors with experience teaching a particular topic likely have some idea what those misconceptions are. The more that instructors interact with students around the topic, the more they will learn about ways in which their students' understanding of the topic is incorrect or incomplete. For a more systematic approach to determining common misconceptions, instructors might analyze student responses to a free-response question to determine common misconceptions and misunderstandings. Instructors might also find information about common misconceptions in the educational literature in their fields. (See Chapter Four for more ideas

on constructing answer choices to clicker questions that surface common misconceptions.)

2. *Demonstrate to students that they are wrong about the question in as dramatic a way as feasible in order to increase their surprise at being wrong.* In a science class, that might mean performing an experiment in the classroom that concretely shows students the correct answer to the question. In other classes, a social experiment using the students themselves might provide proof of a particular result. If nothing else works, most clicker systems allow instructors to designate the correct answer to a question with a check mark or smiley face or some other visual indicator. Showing students the result of their vote and then having one of these indicators appear next to the correct answer can elicit some gasps of astonishment from students when they realize that the popular answer was the wrong one.

3. *Plan for an explanation that is as helpful to the students' understanding as possible.* This usually means explaining not only the correct answer but also why the popular answer is incorrect. Instructors might ask a few students to volunteer their reasons for choosing an incorrect answer prior to the actual explanation. This allows students who are frustrated at answering incorrectly a chance to voice their thoughts on the question. It also provides instructors with information on their students' thoughts about the question, perspectives to which instructors can respond in their explanations.

4. *Having student volunteers share their reasoning for choosing the correct answer to a question can be productive.* This gives the minority of students who answered the question correctly a chance to shine. Also, students are sometimes better able to understand their peers' explanations than the ones that instructors provide.

STRUCTURING CLASS TIME

A classroom response system can be used to structure a class session in ways that help students learn. The think-vote-share activity helps to focus students' attention on a particular question and introduce a time of class discussion. The peer instruction method can provide a useful way to structure an active learning exercise for students, whether that exercise takes two minutes or twenty. Even creating a time for telling provides a certain rhythm in a class session. Some instructors use classroom response systems in other ways to structure portions of class sessions and even entire class sessions.

Case Study: Biological Sciences

Instructors using the case study method of instruction (Barnes, Christensen, & Hansen, 1994; Herreid, 2007) typically provide students with a description of a real or fictional problem or situation. Students are given time to read this case study and respond to a series of questions about it, typically questions that require students to apply knowledge and skills gained in the course thus far to the contextualized problem in the case study. Often students read the case study and respond to the questions prior to class, and class time is spent discussing the case study and associated questions.

Herreid (2006) proposes the use of classroom response systems to facilitate "interrupted case studies." In an interrupted case study, students read and respond to a case study during class. They are initially given only part of the case study and then asked a series of application and critical thinking clicker questions about this first part. Once these questions have been asked, answered, and discussed, they are given another portion of the case study and asked another set of questions. This process continues until the entire case study has been analyzed in class.

Brickman (2006) describes her use of interrupted case studies in a three-hundred-student, introductory biology course. She has students work through case studies in permanent six-person teams. Each team is given a single clicker with which to respond to the questions embedded in the case study. Case studies used in more traditional ways often involve ill-defined problems with multiple reasonable solutions; part of the challenge of the case study is determining what those possible solutions are and evaluating their relative merits. Brickman finds that in her large-enrollment course, less open-ended case studies are more appropriate. As a result, her case studies focus on conceptual understanding and the data analysis skills used frequently in the biological sciences.

WHY USE CLICKERS TO STRUCTURE CLASS TIME?

Most research on attention span (Hartley & Davies, 1978; Midden-dorf & Kalish, 1996) indicates that undergraduate students are able to pay attention for ten to twenty minutes before losing that attention for some amount of time, although some researchers (Wilson & Korn, 2007) dispute this finding. Many instructors see value in structuring a class session into a sequence of activities (mini-lectures, small-group discussions, large-group discussions, individual writing exercises, and so on) as a way to help students maintain their attention during an entire class. The simple act of picking up a clicker and responding to a question can pro-vide the "change-up" in a lecture Middendorf and Kalish (1996) argue is often needed to hold students' attention. Furthermore, some students respond well to kinesthetic activities, which involve movement and tactile sensation. Clickers can facilitate such an activity in a minimal way. Since a quick clicker question can help focus students' attention on the classroom activity in which they should be engaged, clickers can be used several times within a class period to keep students on task. Classroom response systems can be used in a variety of ways to structure class time beyond simply asking quick clicker questions, and are thus often use-ful tools for helping students maintain attention during a class session.

Structuring a class session helps students pay attention, and structures that include activities can also help focus their attention in productive ways on particular tasks. Students who know that they will be asked to respond to a specific question or complete a specific task in the next five, ten, or fifteen minutes are often more likely to engage seriously with classroom activities during that time frame, particularly if they have some indication as to how they will be asked to respond. This can be more productive for some students than the task of taking notes on a sixty-minute lecture with the goal of doing well on an exam three or four or more weeks away. Because all students are asked to respond to a clicker question, they are more likely to be engaged with the activity at hand. Since those responses can be tracked by instructors and tied to student participation grades, students are more likely to take the activity at hand seriously, increasing their focus and engagement.

Clickers can be used as well to gather information from students in order to determine the direction of a class session, giving all students a voice in determining that direction. For example, Robert Bartsch, who teaches psychology at the University of Houston at Clear Lake, likes to ask what he calls "class process" questions. He might ask his students at the start of a class whether they would prefer a lecture or a small-group activity. Hinde and Hunt (2006) suggest a class structure that one might call a "question tree." They give the example of a lesson on government policy options in an economics course. By directing students' attention to a particular policy problem and then asking students to vote on several possible policy choices that might be used to address that problem, an instructor can invite students to determine the focus of subsequent class discussions. Class time is spent exploring the ramifications of the policy choice selected by the most students. Students then vote on other policy choices to explore as time allows.

Hinde and Hunt's question tree is fairly simple, but one can imagine an instructor posing an initial challenge and providing students with a few options as to how to proceed. The instructor then asks the students to vote on their preferred response using their clickers. The most popular choice is then used to shape the next portion of the class session as the instructor and students begin to respond to the challenge in the way suggested by this choice. At some point, another choice is presented to the students, asking them their preference as to the next phase of the analysis of the challenge at hand, and this process repeats itself until the challenge is sufficiently explored. Depending on the nature of the challenge, students might choose responses that lead to dead-ends, requiring the instructor to return to earlier questions and have students select other responses. It would be challenging for an instructor to design a question tree of this sort with branches within branches, but students might find such a tree rather engaging.

MAKING CLASS MORE FUN

Many classroom response systems include features that can be used to add an element of competitive fun to a classroom. For instance, many systems allow instructors to set up teams and track team performance on clicker questions during a class session. Students respond to a clicker question at the start of class that asks them to designate their team number. Then during the class session, students respond to subsequent content questions, typically ones with single correct answers, perhaps conferring with their teammates prior to answering. At the end of class, the system displays the score for each team: the number of correct answers submitted during class by members of that team. The instructor might offer some kind of prize such as candy or extra credit to the team scoring the highest.

Case Study: Mathematics

Meredeth McCoy teaches mathematics courses at Columbia State Community College in Tennessee that students take in preparation for college algebra. Each course typically has between twenty-five and thirty students. McCoy first learned about classroom response systems at a technology fair, and her department purchased a set of clickers for instructors in the department to use. She initially used them for graded quizzes, but this did not seem to engage her students very well. She then tried asking some ungraded clicker questions during her lectures, but this did not quite work either.

What really engaged McCoy's students was one of the competitive games her clicker system facilitated. In each round of this game, each student is assigned one of several questions printed on a handout. Students complete their assigned questions as quickly as they can and submit their answers using their clickers. Then the system displays the fastest responder for each of the questions asked. Students score points for correct answers, and they score bonus points when they are the fastest responders. McCoy finds that this game engages her students because it is competitive but not punitive: students compete to be the fastest responder with a correct answer, but they also receive full points for a correct answer even if they are not first to respond. The fact that students are answering different questions helps prevent cheating, as does the competitive aspect of the game. She finds this game works especially well when helping students prepare for tests.

The description of Parvanak Fassihi's classroom games earlier in this chapter provides another example.

Why Use Clickers to Make Classes Fun?

Although the primary goal of a college or university course is student learning, not fun, a little fun can help students maintain attention and engagement with course activities. As long as any activities designed to add a little fun to a class session are also helping students learn, students are likely to find them enjoyable and productive. Many instructors use these kinds of games to make exam preparation sessions more engaging, for instance.

Also, instructors who help their students enjoy their classes a little more often find that this helps establish a useful rapport with their students. Positive interpersonal interactions can increase students' interest in the subject of a course, interest in engaging productively in course activities designed by their instructor, and willingness to forgive their instructor when he or she makes a mistake or plans an activity that does not turn out well.

Some students find competition motivating. These students engage more seriously with a task when they know they have a chance at outperforming their peers publicly and so enjoy participating in classroom games in which they compete. Other students respond more positively to collaboration and team experiences. These students can thrive in team-based classroom games. Classroom response systems can provide useful technology for supporting these kinds of games. Some students react negatively to high-stakes competition, however, so keeping these kinds of activities low stakes, with no penalty for performing poorly or where the award for performing well is minor, can help make them motivating for more students.

Clickers allow instructors to incorporate elements of popular television game shows into a college or university learning experience. Many game shows use multiple-choice questions or contestants clicking buttons to answer questions quickly, components that can be replicated by clickers. An element of many television game and reality shows is the dramatic "reveal," when the results of some game element, round of voting, or transformation are first displayed to the audience. An instructor with a little flair for the dramatic can use clickers to create similar reveals in the classroom, surprising students with the summary of student responses that clicker systems provide on screen. Furthermore, clickers also provide instant summaries and scoring of student responses. This allows for a more lively and faster-paced game-oriented class sessions.

CHAPTER TWO

ASSESSING STUDENTS WITH CLICKERS

One of the primary functions of a classroom response system is to provide instructors with information on their students' learning. Knowing what students understand and what they do not is useful when it is time to evaluate their performance in a course. It is also useful on a day-to-day basis, providing instructors with information they can use to make teaching choices responsive to student learning needs. Both of these uses of clickers, often called, respectively, *summative* and *formative assessment*, are described in this chapter, beginning with the latter use.

UNCOVERING STUDENT LEARNING

Classroom response systems can be effective tools for uncovering student learning during a class session: discovering what students understand, what they do not understand, and what perspectives they have on important topics. This information enables instructors to respond to what they discover about student learning during that same class session. Beatty, Gerace, Leonard, and Dufresne (2006) call this "agile teaching," and Draper and Brown (2004) refer to it as "contingent teaching." I use *agile teaching* here given the use of the word *contingent* to describe part-time and adjunct instructional positions. This use of classroom response system data dates back at least as far as the 1970s when wired systems were used to generate these data (Judson & Sawada, 2002).

Agile teaching often works as follows. An instructor poses a multiple-choice question and has students think about and respond to it using their clickers. Looking at the summary of student responses generated by the classroom response system, the instructor decides how to proceed. If most of the students answer the question correctly, the instructor might move on to the next question or topic. If some of the students answer the question incorrectly, the instructor can spend more class time on the question by providing a mini-lecture on the question, having students engage in small-group discussion about the question and voting again with their clickers, or engaging in a classwide discussion about the question. When instructors practice agile teaching, class time is spent in ways that are responsive to the students' needs.

Case Study: Environmental Sciences

Thomas Benzing uses clickers in the course on environmental issues in science and technology he teaches at James Madison University. The course typically has fifty students: both first-year students majoring in the sciences and nonmajors of all years. In a typical fifty-minute class period, Benzing might ask between six and eight clicker questions. He often poses a question, has his students respond to the question individually using their clickers, displays the results to the class without indicating the correct answer, then asks for volunteers to explain popular answer choices, which leads to a classwide discussion of the question.

In a lesson on the structure of carbon dioxide molecules, included in the course because of the role these atmospheric molecules play in absorbing infrared light, Benzing first asked his students how many electrons such a molecule has. Answering this question required a straightforward application of knowledge of the periodic table of elements, and about three-fourths of the students answered this question correctly. A subsequent question asked about the kinds of chemical bonds (single and/or double) in the molecule. Only 60 percent answered this more difficult question correctly.

If 90 percent of his students answer a clicker question correctly, Benzing usually moves on to another topic, encouraging the remaining 10 percent to see him during his office hours for additional help. If only 30 percent answer a question correctly, Benzing knows that the question is a difficult one for his students and that he should spend more time on it, diagnosing his students' misconceptions, working through some examples, or asking a follow-up clicker question to identify particular misconceptions.

An advantage Benzing sees in using clickers is that they let him hear from all students who do not understand a particular topic, not only those who are vocal in expressing their confusion. With the clickers, he is better able to respond to the less vocal students who are also confused.

WHY USE CLICKERS TO UNCOVER STUDENT LEARNING?

Using classroom response systems to practice agile teaching is a kind of formative assessment, a term used to describe assessment that provides "feedback to improve teaching and learning" (Bransford, Brown, & Cocking, 2000). Each group of students that takes a particular course is unique in the ways that they learn and understand aspects of the course material. Furthermore, each student within a group of students is unique as well. As a result, the more an instructor can find out about his or her students—what they understand, what they do not understand, and how they learn—the more likely it is that the instructor can tailor instruction to meet the students' unique learning needs. Assessing student learning for this purpose (instead of or in addition to the purpose of evaluating student performance and assigning grades) can provide useful feedback to the instructor.

Sometimes instructors can be surprised by what they learn about their students through formative assessment. Often a particular group of students will find difficult a topic that the instructor assumed they would find easy or vice versa. For example, Charlene Harkins teaches a large-enrollment nutrition course at the University of Minnesota at Duluth. She once asked her students to identify, using their clickers, the infectious diseases among a list of diseases. The correct answer was "none of the above," but many of her students chose heart disease. She thought this would be an easy question for her students, but it was clear from the results displayed that they needed more instruction on this topic.

The anonymity that clickers provide students can sometimes be used to uncover student perspectives that might not be clear to instructors through other means of assessment. For example, Teresa Cosby, who teaches political science at Furman University, was surprised by the results from a clicker question in an upper-level course asking students if the U.S. Supreme Court case *Brown* v. *Board of Education* affected public opinion on race in the United States. During the classwide discussion of this question, most students seemed to think that it had an effect. However, the clicker results showed a split decision, with a relatively large group of students stating that public opinion on race would have changed with or without that particular judicial decision. These students had either remained silent during the prior class discussion or had expressed different views from the ones they expressed through their clickers.

Students also benefit when they are able to determine what they understand, what they do not understand, and how they are learning. This is typically why instructors return student work with comments and suggestions, not just final grades. Students can act on the feedback that instructors give them to improve their learning in a course. Assessing student learning in a formative fashion with clickers not only provides the instructor with useful information, but when students find out whether the answers they submit in response to a clicker question are correct, they are given information they can use to improve their learning and course performance. Furthermore, since a classroom response system can display the distribution of student responses to a clicker question, students can use the feedback to determine how well they understand course material relative to their peers. This can provide a useful motivation for many students.

Instructors learn a lot about what their students understand and with what they struggle by analyzing their performance on midterm exams, papers, and other major assessments in a course. This information can be used following these assessments to provide additional support and further explanations around topics that students find most difficult. However, assessing student learning more frequently through clicker questions can provide similar information on student learning that can be acted on before major assessments are assigned. This helps to prevent instances in which many students are confused by a particular topic early in the semester but the instructor does not discover this until after the first midterm exam. Discovering this kind of confusion earlier in the semester can enable an instructor to deal with confusion in a more timely manner. Clicker questions also allow students to receive feedback on their own learning more frequently, letting them know when they need to seek additional help or other resources. Students often cite this in survey responses as a particularly useful feature of classroom response systems.

Clickers enable instructors to collect information on student learning from all students in a classroom quickly, easily, and simultaneously. Furthermore, classroom response systems automatically summarize this information and report this summary to instructors and students in an easy-to-read bar chart. Other methods of formative assessment typically lack one or more of these advantages. For instance, having students share their answers to questions verbally during class is a quick way to collect information on student learning from students, but usually only a portion of students are able to share their answers in this way, making it difficult for instructors to get a sense of where all of their students stand on a particular topic. Collecting written responses from students to a question posed by the instructor is one way to gather feedback from everyone in a class, but it requires time and effort to analyze that feedback. Usually that feedback cannot be acted on until a subsequent class session. Clickers enable instructors to collect and act on feedback on all of their students' learning within a single class period. In very small classes, instructors have more options for gathering and acting on this kind of feedback. However, even with as few as fifteen students in a class, this can be difficult. Clickers scale up well to larger classes, providing a mechanism for fast, formative assessment in instructional settings where there are often few other options.

Occasions for Formative Assessment Using Clickers

One useful time to conduct formative assessment is at the start of a course, unit, or class. Background knowledge probes (Angelo & Cross, 1993) are classroom assessment techniques designed to assess the knowledge, skills, experiences, and perspectives that students possess as they begin learning a particular topic. Asking a few clicker questions along these lines as a topic is first discussed in class can be an effective way to understand how students are likely to approach the material. This exercise can reveal aspects of the topic that students already understand, aspects that they do not understand as well, and student perspectives on the topic of which the instructor might not be aware.

For example, Thomas Palmeri often uses clickers to assess students' prior knowledge at the beginning of the research methods course he teaches in the Department of Psychology at Vanderbilt University. For instance, he asks his students to report their confidence in computing basic statistics used in his course: means, medians, and standard deviations. He finds that students often overestimate their skills in these clicker questions, but the questions serve to let students know that he expects them to know these skills. When he later reviews these skills, many students then realize they do not know these topics as well as they thought they did.

Weston Dripps teaches earth and environmental science courses at Furman University and often uses clickers to assess his students' understanding of environmental issues at the beginning of units in his courses. For example, he finds that many environmental science topics are referenced in popular culture, particularly in movies. Often these references are only partially accurate, however, and sometimes they are wildly inaccurate, but he finds that students' perceptions about these topics are influenced by their portrayal in popular media, particularly since special effects in movies are so convincing.

Dripps likes to begin a unit on climate change, for instance, by showing a clip from a movie that deals with that subject, such as *The Day After Tomorrow*. He then asks his students a series of questions about the subject, such as the ones in Example 2.1, designed to assess their misconceptions about the subject. He uses the results of these questions to inform his lesson planning for the rest of the unit. Since the misconceptions each class of students possesses differ, the information provided by his classroom response system allows him to plan lessons that address the particular misconceptions of each group of students.

Example 2.1

Question 1. Global warming could lead to the shutdown of the North Atlantic's ocean circulation pattern causing global cooling.

A. Strongly agree

B. Moderately agree

C. Moderately disagree

D. Strongly disagree

Question 2. In response to global warming, more extreme weather events like tornados striking Los Angeles and baseball-size hailstones pummeling Japan are likely.

A. Strongly agree

B. Moderately agree

C. Moderately disagree

D. Strongly disagree

Question 3. If the West Antarctic ice sheet were to melt, how much would the global sea level rise?

A. Less than 1 foot

B. 3 feet

C. 20 feet

D. 100 feet

E. 300 feet

Weston Dripps, Earth and Environmental Sciences, Furman University

Ron McClamrock often uses clickers to conduct background knowledge probes at the beginning of individual class sessions in the philosophy courses he teaches at the State University of New York at Albany. He might pose a question like the one in Example 2.2, which asks students to respond intuitively to a question dealing with a course topic. He uses these questions, which typically do not have correct answers, to motivate his students to engage with these topics and show them that they already have ideas about the topics in his courses. Many of his students initially believe that they could not possibly have something to say about a topic in a philosophy course, and these questions help to dispel that belief. The questions also give McClamrock a sense of his students' preconceived notions about the topics in his courses.

Example 2.2

What do you think of this claim? "Since it's possible that everything we experience is a big, complicated illusion (or a virtual reality simulation), we don't really know anything about the world (like that there are tables and chairs, or that I have a body)."

A. I think that's generally right.

B. I disagree. Even if it's possible that everything we experience is an illusion, that doesn't mean we don't actually know about the external world.

C. I don't think it's at all possible that everything we experience could be an illusion at all.

D. I don't understand, or have no opinion.

E. This convinces me I should have taken English.

Ron McClamrock, Philosophy, State University of New York at Albany

In addition to using clickers to assess student understanding at the beginning of a class session, many instructors use them several times during the session. An instructor might lecture on a particular topic for ten or fifteen minutes, then ask a few clicker questions to find out how well students understood that portion of the lecture. If the class session contains more active learning approaches to instruction, such as small-group or classwide discussions or individual or small-group writing activities, asking clicker questions a few times during the class to see how well students are understanding the topic of the day can be very useful.

Another useful time for agile teaching is during a session devoted to the preparation of students for an upcoming exam or test. Instructors often find it difficult to review all the material from an entire unit in a one- to two-hour review session. Reviewing test material using clicker questions allows instructors to determine the topics for which students are least prepared and to spend limited review session time on those topics. Instructors use clickers in exam review sessions for other purposes as well. For instance, Corly Brooke, who teaches a two-hundred-student human development course at Iowa State University, has her students answer sample exam questions using clickers during her exam review sessions. Her exams consist of multiple-choice questions, and her students often assume that these questions will be relatively easy factual recall questions. Since the questions are usually more difficult application questions, Brooke uses clicker questions during exam review sessions to help her students know what to expect on their exams.

FREQUENTLY ASKED QUESTIONS ABOUT AGILE TEACHING

Gathering systematic feedback on student learning during a class session with a classroom response system can pose some interesting challenges for instructors, particularly those not used to acting on student feedback on the fly during class. Instructors usually plan their class sessions ahead of time, and responding to the results of a clicker question during class can disrupt those plans. The following suggestions offer some options for making the many classroom decisions that arise when responding to the results of clicker questions. The response depends in part on the nature of those results, so the first few questions below consider a few common cases.

The cases that follow assume that the clicker question has at least one correct answer. Chapter Three contains a discussion of student perspective questions that includes suggestions on responding to questions that do not have correct and incorrect answers.

How might an instructor respond if most students answer a clicker question correctly?

Suppose that a large majority of students, perhaps 80 to 100 percent, answer a clicker question correctly. This might be considered reasonably strong evidence that most students understand the question, a positive outcome for a clicker question used for formative assessment. It provides evidence that the students understand the course topic covered by the question at hand and are ready to move on to the next topic in the class session.

However, some students might have simply guessed the correct answer to the question, particularly if the question has only two or three answer choices. (Some instructors include a "not sure" or "I don't know" answer choice to prevent random guessing. See Chapter Four for a discussion of this option.) Students who guessed at the answer might have little understanding of the question. Other students might understand the question sufficiently well to answer it correctly, but might not understand the question as completely as their instructor would like them to. Given these possibilities, hearing from a few students regarding the reasons they chose their answers can provide an instructor with a better sense of the students' level of understanding.

An instructor might start by saying something like, "Answer choice B was the most popular choice. Would someone who chose B mind sharing with the class why they thought that answer choice was correct?" (Phrasing a request in this way does not confirm what the students likely suspect at this point: that the popular answer is the correct one. Students who believe they know the correct answer may be less likely to engage in further discussion of the question, so it is useful to keep students guessing at this point.) If students are reluctant to volunteer, this might be a sign that many of them are not sure of their answers. If an instructor hears from one or more student volunteers but the reasons they provide for their answers are incorrect or incomplete, this too could be a sign that students need more time on the question at hand. If these or other signs lead an instructor to suspect that the students do not understand the question as well as the clicker results might lead one to believe, then he or she might implement one of the strategies described later in this chapter for responding to results that indicate that students find a question unclear.

If an instructor is convinced that most of the students understand the question reasonably well, he or she might reveal the results of the vote to the students (if he or she has not already done so) and confirm for the students that the popular answer was the correct one. The instructor might share an explanation for the question at this point. Students often benefit from hearing each other's explanations, but students also typically want to hear their instructor's take on a question or topic. Angel Hoekstra, who teaches sociology at the University of Colorado at Boulder, conducts research on student perceptions of classroom response systems. Initial results of her research confirm that many students want to hear their instructor's perspective on a question even when most students get the question correct. She recommends instructors do this regularly.

Even when most students answer a question correctly, it is often productive to spend a little time reviewing the question and its answer choices with the students. An explanation helps to strengthen and cement that understanding for students who already understand the question fairly well. For students who are still unclear about the question, the explanation provides them with another chance to understand it. Furthermore, if the minority of students who answered incorrectly are not given a chance to find out why their answers were incorrect, they might not learn as much from the experience and might find the experience discouraging.

Because understanding why certain answer choices are incorrect is often as useful to students as hearing an explanation of a correct answer, instructors might say a few words about each of the incorrect answer choices for the question at hand or have students volunteer some thoughts on the incorrect choices. Since the students who answered the question incorrectly are in the minority, instructors may not be successful in asking for students to volunteer their reasons for choosing incorrect answer choices. However, instructors might ask students to volunteer reasons that some of the incorrect answer choices might seem plausible, as Judson and Sawada (2006) suggest. Another option, suggested by Anthony Crider, who teaches astronomy at Elon University, is to ask a student to explain to the class why he or she ruled out particular answer choices.

In summary, when most students answer a clicker question correctly, it is tempting for instructors to move right along to the next item in the agenda for class that day. However, it is often worth investigating whether students actually understand the question as well as the clicker results would indicate. Also, it is often productive to spend at least a little time reviewing the question and its correct and incorrect answer choices with the students before moving on, perhaps with the instructor offering a few explanations or having a few students share their thoughts with the class.

How might an instructor respond to mixed clicker results?

Suppose that a significant portion of students, perhaps between 30 and 70 percent, answer a clicker question correctly, but the rest of the students do not. Many instructors would view these mixed results as evidence that the question uncovers important student difficulty with the topic. Questions that produce results such as these serve a highly useful purpose in identifying student misconceptions.

One possible response is for an instructor to explain the question, the correct answer, and the incorrect answers to the students. (As noted above, it is often important to spend as much time explaining incorrect answer choices as it is explaining the correct one.) This response is a fairly efficient way to provide some support to students having difficulties with the question. Students who know or suspect that they have answered the question incorrectly are likely to pay attention to these sorts of explanations. Students who know they have answered the question correctly may be a little less inclined to follow these explanations, so it can be helpful for instructors to delay confirmation of the correct answer for a time during these explanations.

Since a classroom response system lets an instructor know how many students choose each of the incorrect answers but does not tell instructors why students choose these answers, it can be helpful to have a few students share their reasons for their answers with the class before providing an explanation of the question and its answer choices. The misconceptions, partial understandings, and perspectives on the question that students share can provide instructors with useful qualitative information about their learning that instructors can use to tailor an explanation of the question and its answer choices to their students' unique difficulties with the question. Without hearing from some students, any explanation an instructor provides rests on assumptions about the precise nature of the students' understanding of the topic, and instructors run the risk that those assumptions are incorrect.

However, since the clicker results such as these reveal that the question is a difficult one for students, students might need to spend more time and effort thinking about it. Instructor explanations of the correct and incorrect answers to the question might not engage students in this thinking sufficiently, since some will simply listen to such explanations without thinking about them very deeply. Thus, another response to mixed results from a clicker question is to facilitate a classwide discussion of the question, one with the goal of helping students arrive at a correct answer by weighing the various arguments their peers make about the question and its answer choices. This approach involves more active engagement on the students' part and can help many students construct a more complete understanding of the question than if they listened to an explanation of it. (See the section on generating classwide discussions in Chapter One for suggestions for leading this kind of discussion.)

The responses described thus far—explaining the question with or without first hearing from students or leading a classwide discussion of the question—are relatively time-efficient ways to help students understand the correct answer and provide some support for them to resolve any difficulties they have with the question. However, unless an instructor has a second clicker question on the same topic prepared, he or she might find it difficult to determine if the explanations given or the classwide discussion of the question makes sense to students. (A second clicker question on the same topic, prepared ahead of time or constructed on the fly, is a useful way to assess what students learned from the discussion of the first question.)

Another set of responses to mixed clicker results is to have the students reengage with the question in some fashion, then have them answer the question again with their clickers, submitting the same or different answers than they did the first time. Often, but not always, a greater proportion of students will answer the question correctly on a second vote after a period of further consideration of the question. These approaches can take more class time, but they often offer students additional opportunities to arrive at correct answers on their own. They also provide instructors a way to assess the extent to which student understanding of a clicker question and its associated topic improves as a result of further class time spent on that question. Options for having students reengage with the clicker question include the following:

1. Ask students to discuss the question in pairs or small groups. The success of this peer instruction lies in the ability of students with the correct answer and, more important, correct reasons for that answer to explain the question to their peers. (See Chapter One for more reasons for using this approach, as well as suggestions for implementing it.)

2. If the students have already discussed the question in pairs or small groups, one option is to have the pairs or small groups combine into double-sized groups to continue their discussion of the question. This means that students will likely encounter new perspectives on the question from members of their larger groups, making it more likely that more students will sharpen their reasoning on the question. Brian Augustine, who teaches chemistry at James Madison University, suggests a slightly different approach: instructing students to form new small groups for a second round of peer instruction.

3. A fairly quick way to have students reconsider the question is to provide them with one or more hints about the question or a brief mini-lecture on the topic of the question, one that provides new information or reminds students of pertinent information they have already seen without giving away the answer to the question. With a little additional information, students may be able to reconsider the question in productive ways. For example, Stacy Klein, who teaches biomedical engineering courses at Vanderbilt University, sometimes has students respond to a question individually and then discuss the question in small groups and respond a second time. This usually increases the number of students answering correctly, but if a significant number of students are still unsure of the correct answer, she might provide some numerical data in the form of a chart or graph that supports the correct answer and then have the students respond again using their clickers. This gives the students who did not answer correctly on the second try another chance to understand the question, and she finds that the students who answered correctly earlier in the process appreciate it when they see data that confirm their intuition about a question.

4. A similar option is to eliminate one of the answer choices for the students, explaining why that answer choice is incorrect. Students who initially chose the eliminated answer choice will have to select other answers on a subsequent vote, and the explanation of the eliminated answer choice might encourage other students to reconsider their answers as well.

5. For each of the more popular answer choices, ask for a student volunteer to share reasons for choosing that answer. This method can help students reconsider answer choices they did not select initially. Sometimes students find the student volunteer who explains the correct answer so persuasive that a second vote is unnecessary. In these instances, it is often clear from verbal and nonverbal cues that as soon as the correct explanation for the question is voiced, most students who had initially chosen incorrect answers realize their errors. However, for questions that students find difficult, having a few students share their lines of thought with the entire class helps move some students in the right direction, but does not give away the answer for them.

6. For challenging questions, it is sometimes possible to facilitate a classwide discussion about the question without confirming the correct answer for the students. By limiting instructor comments and relying primarily on students to carry this discussion, students can explore perspectives on the question they had not initially considered, potentially leading more of them to the correct answer. This kind of discussion is difficult to lead, since the goal is not to arrive at the correct answer but rather to explore the question in ways that help students arrive at the correct answer themselves. (See the section on generating classwide discussions in Chapter One for more advice on facilitating these kinds of discussions.)

If, after further engagement with the question and a second vote, students are still unclear about the question at hand, instructors might have them engage with the question again but in a different way, before a third vote. For instance, instructors might have students reflect on and answer the question individually, discover that only a relatively small portion of them answer the question correctly, have them then engage in peer instruction about the question, and respond again with their clickers. If the percentage of correct answers is still low after this second vote, instructors might drop a few hints about the question, then have the students return to their small groups for further discussion and a third vote. If the third vote still does not result in most students answering the question correctly, instructors might have a few students volunteer their reasoning for the entire class to hear, then have the students vote a fourth time. For questions that students find very challenging, multiple interactions and multiple votes may be required to help them fully understand the question.

How might an instructor respond if most students answer a clicker question incorrectly?

Suppose that a large majority of students, perhaps 80 to 100 percent, answers a given clicker question incorrectly. This is fairly conclusive proof that the students do not understand the question, although it is possible that an error in the question is the reason so many students answered incorrectly. Assuming the question is worded correctly, then a result such as this one argues for spending more class time, either immediately or in the future, on the topic at hand.

The reengagement strategies mentioned above as possible responses to mixed clicker results can be useful here as well. Having students discuss the question in small groups, providing a few hints about the question, eliminating an answer choice, having a few students share their reasoning with the entire class, and leading a class discussion about the question can help students engage more deeply with the question and reconsider their initial answers. However, some of these strategies may be less effective given the apparent difficulty of the question and the scarcity of students who answered it correctly.

For example, if only 5 or 10 percent of students answer a question correctly, having them discuss the question further in small groups might not be useful. In that case, most of the small groups would consist entirely of students confused about the question. Sometimes this can work well: two students with different wrong answers can put their heads together and come up with the correct answer. Dennis Jacobs, who teaches chemistry at the University of Notre Dame, has documented this phenomenon in his research on peer instruction. However, if the question is as challenging as the initial clicker results would indicate, having students discuss the question among themselves might not help them make progress on understanding. Instructors might see the percentage of correct answers rise only slightly.

If few students answered the question correctly on the initial vote, then it can be very helpful for an instructor to provide a few hints about the question or to spend a little time lecturing on the topic of the question before having the students vote again. Results such as these indicate that students do not understand the topic and may not be able to improve their answers to the question without some insight into that topic from their instructor. Providing additional direct instruction, then having the student answer the question again with their clickers, can be a useful response.

In some cases, instructors might not want the students to reengage with the question and answer it again with their clickers. An instructor might not think it likely that the students' performance on the question will improve or might not want to spend class time in this way. In these cases, one option is to share the initial clicker results with the students and let them know that most of them answered the question incorrectly. This information, particularly if the correct answer can be demonstrated conclusively for the students, can prepare them to want to listen and understand an explanation of the question and its answer choices. (See the section on creating times for telling in Chapter One for more on this approach.)

Instructors might also find that students' poor showing on a clicker question indicates such a fundamental misunderstanding of the topic that they do not feel that they can adequately address this misunderstanding immediately. These instructors might prefer to return to the topic in a subsequent class period after they have had time to plan an appropriate response. Instructors selecting this option are likely to find it helpful to have a few students share their reasons for their answers, which provides the instructor with a richer understanding of the students' misunderstandings. Some students might grumble at a decision to defer a conclusive discussion of a confusing question, so instructors might choose to spend a little time discussing the answer to the question while also letting students know that they will return to the topic in a subsequent class session.

How might instructors use a question with multiple correct answers, some of which may be more or less reasonable, for formative assessment?

Sometimes it can be productive to ask students to select the best answer to a question from a set of answer choices consisting of several answers that have merit. These one-best-answer questions (Case & Swanson, 2002) are often used to help students develop their critical thinking skills since answering these questions requires students to evaluate the strengths and weaknesses of several possible responses. Sometimes a one-best-answer question has a single answer choice that is conclusively superior to the others; at other times, any one of several answers could be considered best depending on the criteria used to evaluate them. (See Chapter Three for examples of one-best-answer questions.)

Aside from their use in providing students opportunities to practice and develop their critical thinking skills, one-best-answer questions can also be used for formative assessment purposes. Suppose such a question has three reasonably correct answer choices and two answer choices that are verifiably incorrect. It can be useful for an instructor to know that, for instance, 85 percent of the students in a class picked one of the three correct answers since that implies that most of the students understood the question to some extent. However, it can be even more important to know how many students selected each of the three correct answers, a distribution that a classroom response system can provide. That distribution can indicate to an instructor the ways in which students evaluated the answer choices to the question. However, since one-best-answer questions are usually asked out of an interest in students' critical thinking skills, once the distribution of answers to such a question is known, it is often even more useful to have a few students share their reasons for their selections. Thus, often with these questions, it is the small-group and classwide discussion that follows a clicker vote that provides more qualitative and more useful feedback on students' learning.

Depending on the responses to a one-best-answer question submitted by student clickers and on the reasons they provide for their responses by small-group or classwide discussion, an instructor might determine that the students need to spend more time engaging with the question. The reengagement strategies described above in the case of mixed clicker results are often very useful for having students think more deeply about a one-best-answer question. Even if the distribution of student answers does not change between the vote before a reengagement activity and the vote after the activity, it is quite possible for students' arguments for and against various answer choices to improve from the first vote to the second one.

In addition, just as instructors asking questions with single correct answers must decide when during the discussion of a question to tell students which of the answers to the question is correct, instructors asking one-best-answer questions must often decide when to tell students that the question at hand does not have a single correct answer. Since students often expect multiple-choice questions to have single correct answers, they can find one-best-answer questions disconcerting, particularly when the choice of best answer depends on the set of criteria used to evaluate its answer choices. Instructors might tell students that a given question has multiple correct answers before the students respond to the question. This approach can be used to focus students' attention on the evaluative aspects of responding to the question. Alternately, instructors might not reveal to students that a question has multiple correct answers until after the students have responded. This can surprise some students, but if they are given the chance to discuss the question further after knowing that multiple answers have merit, this approach can help them understand that not all questions are as straightforward as they might expect.

When should instructors move on to the next topic?

Instructors sometimes find it difficult to decide when during a class session to move from one topic to the next. One advantage to asking clicker questions in class is that instructors are provided with actual data on which to base this decision. More frequently, instructors rely on their intuitions to make those decisions.

Something about the bar chart that displays the results of a clicker question causes some instructors anxiety regarding decisions to move on to subsequent topics. This is particularly true of questions with single correct answers. Certainly if 100 percent of the students in a class answer a question correctly, the argument can be made that it is time to move on. And if no student answers a question correctly, it is safe to say that students need more time with the topic. However, where might an instructor draw the line between these two cases—90 percent? 80 percent? 70 percent?

Few instructors seem to have hard-and-fast targets they attempt to achieve before moving on. Instead, most consider a variety of factors. Is the topic of the question one that students should master at a given point in the class session or course? Or is it a topic that they will return to in the future in order to refine their understanding? The former argues for spending more time on a question in order to promote mastery learning. The latter argues for moving on and returning to the topic in a subsequent clicker question. The decision to move on also depends on the amount of assistance an instructor wants to provide students on the topic. An instructor may find that only 70 percent of students answer a question correctly and decide to move on to the next topic, challenging the remaining 30 percent to take the initiative to understand the question on their own or seek help during office hours. Moving on also depends on what comes after the question at hand. If the next topic depends on a thorough understanding of the topic, then it might be worth spending more time on the question.

Instructors should also consider the level of engagement of their students. Having a cohort of students who refuse to engage meaningfully in a course can mean that an instructor might never have more than, say, 80 percent of students respond correctly to a clicker question. Knowing students' engagement and motivation levels can be important in interpreting the results of a clicker question.

What should instructors do about students who answer incorrectly when it is time to move on?

One of the great advantages of using a classroom response system in teaching is that clicker questions, particularly those with

answer choices constructed intentionally to surface student misconceptions, allow an instructor to determine which difficulties
and misconceptions are troubling the most students. Suppose that
on a particular clicker question, students who select the incorrect
answer B are likely to do so because of a particular misconception.
If an instructor poses this question to a class and a large number of
students select answer B, then the instructor can confidently spend
some class time discussing the misconception associated with that
answer. Since class time is relatively limited—most college and university courses on a semester system meet only three or four hours
in a week—spending that class time wisely is important. Clickers
provide instructors with information that enables them to use class
time efficiently, responding to the difficulties and misconceptions
that challenge the largest number of students in a class.

However, suppose in this example that students who select C,
also an incorrect answer, do so because of some other misconception, not the one associated with answer B. If an instructor
poses this question to a class and only a small number of students
select answer C, then he or she might confidently spend little
class time discussing the misconception associated with choice C.
Since very few students appear to possess that misconception, an
instructor might argue that relatively little class time should be
spent addressing that misconception in an effort to spend class
time as efficiently as possible.

In practice, the situation is often more complicated. Each
student in a class can approach a particular clicker question
in a unique way. One student might have a slightly different
misconception that leads him to select answer B—one that is
not addressed completely in a discussion of answer B. Another
student might not be able to resolve the misconception that led
her to select answer C in the small amount of time an instructor
spends discussing that choice. The results of a clicker question
can help an instructor spend class time resolving the difficulties
and misconceptions of a majority of students, but there are often
students who have misconceptions or questions about a topic that
go unresolved during a class session.

Using the idea of a "long tail" popularized by Anderson
(2004), one can imagine a bar graph in which each bar represents the frequency of a particular misconception or question

FIGURE 2.1. LONG TAIL OF STUDENT MISCONCEPTIONS AND QUESTIONS.

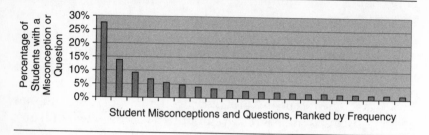

Student Misconceptions and Questions, Ranked by Frequency

students might have about a topic. If these misconceptions and questions are ordered by frequency, with the more commonly occurring misconceptions and questions on the left and less commonly occurring ones on the right, the resulting bar graph might look like the one in Figure 2.1. (The bar graph in Figure 2.1 is a hypothetical one. Generating an actual bar graph of this kind would require systematic research on student learning. The shape of such a bar chart might be quite different from the shape of this one.) A classroom response system is a useful tool in part because it enables an instructor to determine which misconceptions and questions belong on the left side of such a bar graph. Using class time to resolve these commonly occurring misconceptions and questions is an efficient use of time. However, what can an instructor do to help students with misconceptions and questions that appear in the long tail of this bar chart? Although there may not be a silver bullet that addresses this challenge completely, instructors have a variety of practices to draw on to address the needs of these students.

One commonly used option is to invite students who still have questions after a class discussion to see the instructor after class or in office hours. Even when students do not take instructors up on such an offer, the offer itself can help prevent students from being discouraged.

Many instructors post clicker questions to their course Web sites or online course management systems in order to provide students with opportunities to reflect further on the questions. Some instructors indicate the correct answers to these questions when they make them available so that students can check their understanding. Some prefer not to indicate correct answers when posting clicker questions after class so that students who struggle with those questions will be motivated to take advantage of office hours or help sessions in order to discuss the material. Other instructors post brief or full explanations of the correct answers to their clicker questions after class so that students can review and study them. There is some evidence (Bunce, VandenPlas, & Havanki, 2006) that making clicker questions available for student review after class is critically important to the impact such questions can have on student learning.

Audio-recording a class session in which clicker questions are discussed and making that recording available to students after class is another option. Podcast and lecture-capture technologies can make this possibility relatively straightforward for some instructors.

Instructors are advised to watch for students who consistently answer clicker questions incorrectly. There are a variety of reasons a student might regularly miss clicker questions, but such students can often become discouraged and stop trying. (See the discussion of student responses to the use of clickers in Chapter Four for additional thoughts on such students.)

Two Advanced Techniques

Following are descriptions of two ways to practice agile teaching that require perhaps a bit more thinking on one's feet than the ways already described. The first technique, question-driven instruction, comes from the physics community. The second, the use of a multiple-choice question as a backchannel by which students can express their level of understanding or confusion during a lecture, is listed as an advanced technique here because it seems to be rarely used by instructors, although its use with wired classroom response systems dates back at least far as the 1970s (Judson & Sawada, 2002).

Question-Driven Instruction. Beatty, Leonard, Gerace, and Dufresne (2006) propose a form of agile teaching they call *question-driven instruction.* In this approach, lesson plans consist entirely of clicker questions. Which questions are asked depends on how students respond during class. An instructor might come to class with a stack of clicker questions with multiple questions on each topic to be addressed during the class session. As students perform well on clicker questions, the instructor moves on to questions on new topics. As students perform poorly, the instructor asks further questions on the same topic. The instructor does not have a lesson plan in the traditional sense when using this approach. Instead, the course of the class session is determined reactively to demonstrated student learning needs. Peer instruction and classwide discussion are used throughout the class session to help students master course content and develop critical reasoning skills. The question-driven instruction approach might not appeal to every instructor, but those who enjoy thinking on their feet might find it a useful approach.

Backchannel. Another possible approach to gathering formative feedback from students is to pose a question such as, "How well do you understand the lecture thus far?" Answer choices might range from "1. I'm following everything" to "5. Nothing makes sense." An instructor might open this question for student responses and leave it open during the entire class session. Assuming that students can change their response to the question at any time and that the instructor can monitor the responses while the question is still open for responses, then this kind of question provides a useful way for instructors to find out when during a lecture they should slow down and request questions from students.

One can imagine introducing a difficult topic in the lecture and watching the responses to this question spike in the direction of "5. Nothing makes sense." Some classroom response systems provide custom tools for this type of assessment activity, including ones that display the average student response on a line graph that changes in real time like a heart-rate monitor. Classroom response systems that allow free-response questions, not just multiple-choice questions, can be used effectively in this fashion, functioning as a backchannel by which students can submit questions and comments during a lecture. (See the section on free-response questions in Chapter Three for more on this approach.)

EVALUATING STUDENT LEARNING

Classroom response systems can provide both instructors and students with useful information about what and how students are learning in the classroom. This information can be used for formative assessment, but it can also be used for summative assessment—assessment that "measures what students have learned at the end of some set of learning activities" (Bransford et al., 2000). This form of assessment is typically conducted for the purposes of evaluating student learning through graded activities. Many instructors use classroom response systems to automate the grading of quizzes and tests, saving them time and effort. However, clickers can also help instructors turn graded activities into opportunities for formative assessment.

An instructor might use clickers to facilitate an in-class quiz. The instructor poses a series of questions, and students submit answers to those questions using clickers as they are posed. The system automatically grades the students' work based on the instructor's specification of the correct answers to the questions. The instructor then determines which questions were most missed by the students and reviews those in class immediately following the quiz. Some classroom response systems have student-paced modes that allow students to answer questions asynchronously. With these systems, the instructor might distribute a printed copy of the quiz. Then each student submits answers at his or her own pace, even answering the questions out of order if desired. Either way, the classroom response system saves the instructor time in grading and allows the quiz to be reviewed while its questions are still fresh in the minds of students.

Case Study: Health and Physical Education

Lori Paluti uses clickers in the fitness walking and aerobic kickboxing courses she teaches at the Community College of Allegheny County in Pennsylvania. These courses carry two or three credit-hours, so they have both academic and gym components. The courses are small, usually with eight to twelve students each, and many students take them to fulfill a requirement in the nursing program.

Paluti uses clickers primarily for in-class quizzes. She poses a multiple-choice quiz question, gives all her students time to answer the question, displays the bar chart and correct answer, and then moves on to the next question. Her questions tend to focus on the skills she teaches as well as basic wellness concepts. She finds that her students are often easily bored by pencil-and-paper quizzes, but are usually technologically savvy and interested in gadgets. Using clickers for quizzes, even though no small-group or classwide discussion is involved, helps these students engage with her courses and perform better on quizzes. Displaying the results of clicker quiz questions helps build a sense of community among the students, which often motivates them to do well on quizzes. The students appreciate getting instant feedback on their work instead of having to wait days for quizzes to be graded and returned. The clickers help her quizzes feel to her students a little like a game, which helps them stay engaged.

Usually more than half of Paluti's students answer her quiz questions correctly. She finds that the simpler the question stem and answer choices are, the better the students do. She also appreciates that her classroom response system makes it easy to see which questions were the toughest for students, enabling her to respond more directly to their learning needs. Determining that with pencil-and-paper quizzes is possible, but consumes more of her time and energy.

Why Use Clickers to Evaluate Student Learning?

Assigning grades to student work allows instructors to communicate to students and others the level of mastery students achieve in a particular course. Higher grades represent higher levels of mastery, and so grades provide a way of ranking and comparing student performance in a course or sequence of courses. In addition, many students are motivated, for better or for worse, by a desire to obtain high grades. Instructors can leverage this motivation by assigning grades to various forms of student work. For example, a graded in-class quiz on the previous night's reading assignment motivates students to complete that assignment. Any type of graded in-class quiz motivates students to attend and participate. Assigning grades to activities that promote learning and effective study skills can be a productive way to make use of this motivator.

Use of a classroom response system can improve the speed and efficiency with which instructors collect, grade, and record student performance on quizzes and other summative assessments. Furthermore, many instructors have various kinds of attendance policies, and student attendance data can be automatically tracked when clickers are used. Moreover, since classroom response systems can automatically grade student responses, it is possible to determine immediately following a clicker-facilitated quiz which questions most students missed, as well as the most common wrong answers. This information allows instructors to review quizzes immediately following their completion, while the questions are still fresh in students' minds. Without clickers, quizzes often need to be graded and analyzed between classes, delaying the review of the material until subsequent class sessions when the students' perspectives on the quiz questions are not as fresh. Feedback on student learning is useful to students; timely feedback is even more useful.

If students are required to purchase their own clickers and perceive that the rationale for clicker use in a course is to save the instructor's time in collecting and grading responses to quizzes and exams, then students are likely to grumble, perhaps publicly, about the cost of clickers. Why should they spend money to make the instructor's life easier? If instead they perceive that the use of clickers provides some direct benefit to them, they are less likely to object to their use. For example, if students see that clickers used for in-class quizzes allow instructors to let students know their grades more quickly and review those quizzes during class, then students are more likely to perceive the clickers as worth the cost. If students see that clickers used for in-class exams allow instructors to grade multiple-choice portions of those exams more quickly and to spend more time providing meaningful feedback on free-response portions of those exams, then students will be less likely to object to the use of clickers.

Since each student response to each quiz question is tracked in a classroom response system, most systems can provide an item-by-item analysis of a quiz, letting instructors know how many students choose each of the answer choices to each question. These data can be analyzed and used on the fly during class immediately following the quiz. They can also be analyzed after the class session in which the quiz was given to aid instructors in identifying student misunderstandings and formulate additional learning experiences designed to help address these misunderstandings. Looking for patterns across a set of quiz responses can often provide useful insight into how students learn, and often these patterns can be shared productively with colleagues. Without using clickers or some other tool with automatic grading and record-keeping features, it is often difficult and time-consuming to obtain such data on student learning.

Case Study: Biological Sciences

Mary Burke teaches a microbiology course at Oregon State University. The upper-level course typically enrolls 160 students, mostly biology, premedicine, and nursing majors, many of whom have taken organic chemistry and cell biology courses.

Burke uses a classroom response system to facilitate in-class exams. She hands out different versions of an exam to her students. Students enter their exam version number in their clickers as well as their answers to the multiple-choice questions. The response system that Burke uses allows students to answer questions at their own pace and in any order they wish and to change their responses to questions already answered. Burke has her students circle their answers on the printed copy of the exam as a backup in case of technical problems. Her students also respond to a few essay questions in writing. These questions are not handled by her classroom response system.

After class, Burke transfers each student's exam grade from her classroom response system to the student's printed exam copy, which she returns in the next class session. She also posts an answer key to the exam in her online course management system so that her students can compare their answers (circled on the printed copy of the exam) with the correct ones as they prepare for subsequent exams.

IDEAS FOR SUMMATIVE ASSESSMENT USING CLICKERS

Following are descriptions of several different types of graded assignments that can be facilitated by classroom response systems, as well as suggestions for instructors interested in implementing these assignments.

Reading Quizzes. In many courses, students are expected to complete reading assignments before class so that they can draw on those readings as they participate in a class session. One way to encourage students to complete reading assignments is to administer a reading quiz using clickers at the start of a class session. Even asking very straightforward questions about the reading can motivate students to complete reading assignments. Administering such a quiz allows an instructor to collect and grade student responses quickly and efficiently and to review the results of the quiz with the students before moving on to the rest of the class session. These results can help shape the remainder of the class session as the instructor responds to expressed student difficulties with the reading.

Corly Brooke uses clickers to facilitate graded reading quizzes in her human development course at Iowa State University. She gives her students five-question quizzes eight times during the semester. She announces the quizzes ahead of time, and each student is allowed to bring one page of notes for use during each quiz. Combined, the quizzes constitute 10 percent of the students' course grades. Brooke finds that these quizzes work "like nothing else" to motivate students to complete course readings. Her students also indicate that they like having the accountability the quizzes provide.

Elizabeth Cullingford uses graded clicker questions to motivate students in her course on the masterworks of British literature at the University of Texas at Austin to complete course readings. Prior to the first exam in her course, she asks her students a few questions at the start of each class session. One question usually requires students to recall information from the previous lecture, another asks students to recall something from the reading assignment, and a third is designed to test students' close reading skills. This third question is typically more difficult than the first two. Cullingford finds that these clicker questions motivate her students to keep up with the readings for the course until the first exam, at which point it is clear to most students how important the readings are to their performance in the course.

Kori Street uses reading quizzes in her upper-level history seminar courses at Mount Royal College. She asks a series of basic questions about the reading assignment at the start of each class session. Students who do not answer a sufficient number of these questions correctly are told to leave the class session immediately and complete the reading assignment. Since classwide discussion of the readings is such an important component of Street's seminar courses, she finds it critical that students come to class having prepared properly by completing reading assignments. Her reading quizzes work very well to ensure this, ending any problems with students not doing the reading within the first two weeks of class. Her students react positively to her reading quizzes since they force their peers to read, deepening the quality of class discussions. The quizzes also give them feedback on their reading comprehension. Her students do not find her system punitive since it does not lower their grades as long as they are prepared for class.

Homework Quizzes. Another useful quiz to administer using clickers at the start of class is a homework quiz. At the end of one class session, an instructor might give students a set of questions to answer as homework before the next class session. Then at the start of the next session, the instructor poses these same questions to the students as clicker questions. As with reading quizzes, homework quizzes conducted in this fashion allow instructors to grade student responses quickly and to review the results of the quiz immediately after collecting responses. These quizzes are fairly quick to administer, since students formulate answers to the questions before class begins.

Stacy Klein, for instance, often asks clicker questions about her students' homework assignments at the beginning of her courses in biomedical engineering at Vanderbilt. She finds that these questions motivate her students to complete their homework, in part because they know they will be held accountable for it and in part because they know the homework will be discussed during class in the context of these quizzes. Some classroom response systems allow students to store answers to questions in their clicker's internal memory, then submit those answers in a batch once they arrive in class. This speeds up the in-class response collection.

Exams. Classroom response systems with student-paced modes can also be used to facilitate longer assessments, such as tests and exams. Facilitating longer assessments with systems that lack student-paced modes can be difficult, since such systems require all students to respond to a given question before any student can respond to a subsequent one. This synchronous response mode can work well for shorter assessments, but for longer assessments, an asynchronous mode is helpful. Or students could take a more traditional exam, writing down their answers as they complete questions, then submitting all of their answers synchronously and in sequence at the end of class, but this can be time-consuming.

Karina Kline-Gabel, who teaches Spanish language courses at James Madison University, uses a classroom response system with a student-paced mode for exams. Kline-Gabel's exams often consist of multiple-choice questions that focus on grammar and vocabulary, followed by free-response questions that assess students' second-language writing skills. Her students respond to the multiple-choice questions first, using the classroom response system's student-paced mode to allow students to submit their responses asynchronously. Once they complete these questions, they move on to the writing portion of the exam. Kline-Gabel finds that ordering the exam in this way allows the multiple-choice questions to warm up the students for the writing portion. She is sometimes surprised at how poorly her students perform on her multiple-choice questions. She finds that using multiple-choice questions to assess these skills prevents her from being too generous with partial credit, allowing her to grade questions about fundamentals more strictly. This encourages her students to answer multiple-choice questions more carefully, a useful skill since many of these students go on to take multiple-choice exams to obtain entrance to graduate and professional schools.

The classroom response system that Kline-Gabel uses to administer her exams allows her to monitor students' responses as they submit them with their clickers. This feature lets her know when a student has skipped a question. She can then walk over to the student and let the student know. Another reason Kline-Gabel and her students like using the classroom response system for exams is that it automates the grading of the multiple-choice portion of the exam, providing Kline-Gabel with more time to focus on grading the written portion of the exam. She can then return her tests more quickly and provide more timely feedback to students.

She often uses the data from the clicker portion of her exams to guide her review of the exams with the students when returning them. When the students can see that so many of them missed a particular problem, they understand the need for her to spend class time reviewing that topic.

CHAPTER THREE

A TAXONOMY OF CLICKER QUESTIONS

Since classroom response systems allow instructors to rapidly collect and analyze student responses to questions they ask during class, the use and effectiveness of clickers depend heavily on the nature of the questions. This chapter describes a variety of types of questions to ask students during class that take advantage of the engagement and assessment functions provided by clickers and described in Chapters One and Two.

Asking students questions during class is not new to college and university teaching. Instructors routinely ask open-ended and rhetorical questions of their students during class and elicit responses from individual students. Clickers change this dynamic by allowing instructors to receive responses from all students in a class, not just the handful who volunteer or are called on to respond. Instructors used to asking verbal questions of their students often find that this feature of clickers opens the door to different kinds of in-class questions.

All classroom response systems allow instructors to collect responses to multiple-choice questions asked during class. (Some also allow instructors to collect responses to free-response questions.) Asking multiple-choice questions is not a new idea in college teaching either. Many instructors ask multiple-choice questions on tests and exams, and entry exams such as the Graduate Record Examinations and licensure exams, such as the bar examinations taken by prospective lawyers, feature multiple-choice questions as well. However, clickers enable instructors to collect and analyze responses to multiple-choice questions during class, not just after tests have been handed in at the end of a class session. This rapid feedback feature means that types of questions that would not be appropriate on tests and exams can be useful to ask during class with clickers. It also means that clickers can be used not only to assess student learning, but also to engage students in the learning process. In contrast, multiple-choice questions on quizzes and exams are used primarily, if not exclusively, for assessment purposes.

Experience asking questions of students during class without clickers and experience writing multiple-choice test questions can certainly assist instructors in crafting effective in-class clicker questions. However, crafting clicker questions that engage students with course material during class and provide useful instant feedback on student learning and student perspectives is a different task from crafting questions used in other contexts. The examples of clicker questions in this chapter are meant to inspire instructors to use creative questions that leverage the unique characteristics of clickers to help them meet their course goals. Most clicker questions fall into one of two categories: *content questions* used to directly assess student learning and *process questions* used to gather information from students helpful in shaping how students interact with each other and the course material. Most of the questions described here are multiple-choice since these are more commonly used with clickers and since such questions are often more difficult to write.

What follows is not a comprehensive guide to all the different kinds of clicker questions that instructors might ask, nor is it a guide to writing effective multiple-choice questions. Case and Swanson (2002) provide an example of the latter type of guide. Chapter Four also provides some suggestions for crafting clicker questions. However, instructors are likely to find ideas here for types of clicker questions they have not used previously.

Content Questions

Content questions directly assess students' learning. They focus on course content and often have correct and incorrect answers. They range from straightforward questions asking students to recall facts to critical thinking questions that require students to evaluate various answer choices against discipline-specific standards of evidence.

RECALL QUESTIONS

Recall questions ask students to remember facts, concepts, or procedures relevant to a class session or course. They do not assess students' understanding of these facts, concepts, or procedures, merely their memory of them. For instance, in an aerobic kickboxing course at the Community College of Allegheny County, health and physical education instructor Lori Paluti asks her students the question in Example 3.1. This question asks students to recall an aspect of an exercise procedure they have studied during class. Ivan Shibley asks students in his chemistry courses at Penn State Berks the recall question, "Which of the following is a metalloid: C, Al, Zn, Te, or Na?" This question tests his students' recall of a system used to classify elements.

Example 3.1

To which position do your hands return after throwing an offensive punch?

A. Guard

B. Pyramid

C. Resting

Lori Paluti, Health and Physical Education, Community College of Allegheny County

Recall questions are typically used more for assessing student learning than engaging students in a class session. These questions often do not generate productive classwide or small-group discussions. Students either remember the answers to these questions or they do not. An instructor could, however, use a recall question to motivate discussions about how students choose to go about remembering important facts in a course. The point of such a discussion would not be to examine the particular factual recall question, but instead to discuss more general study skills.

Recall questions are commonly used on pencil-and-paper quizzes and tests to assess student recall, but these questions can serve other useful functions as in-class clicker questions. Asking students at the beginning of a class to recall facts, concepts, or procedures from preclass readings, previous class sessions in the same course, or previous courses can be a useful way to help students prepare for the class at hand and determine what they might need to review before proceeding. Often students need to know certain facts about a topic or procedure before they can proceed with deeper understanding, analysis, or application of that topic or procedure. Recall clicker questions can be used to make sure students have this base knowledge before proceeding with more complex tasks.

Recall questions that students perceive as easy can also help build student confidence. If students are consistently struggling with more difficult clicker questions, asking a few easy recall questions can give students a break and remind them that there is some material that they know.

Recall questions asked of students who have access to their notes, a textbook, or the Internet may not serve their intended purpose. If students are able to find the answer to a factual question using these kinds of sources, then the question does not actually test their recall. For example, inserting a recall question after ten or fifteen minutes of lecture that students can answer by scanning through the notes they just took on the lecture and finding a key word assesses only the students' ability to maintain attention and take useful notes. This can serve the useful purpose of encouraging students to pay attention and take notes, but it does not assess their recall of course material.

In some courses, such as some anatomy courses that medical and veterinary students take, it is vitally important that students remember certain key facts, concepts, or procedures. Recall questions can be very useful in these courses. In other courses, memorization of facts, concepts, and procedures functions primarily as a necessary foundation for more complex student learning goals. Many courses feature student learning goals at the higher levels of Bloom's taxonomy of educational objectives. The most recent version of this taxonomy (Anderson & Krathwohl, 2001) identifies six basic cognitive processes involved in learning: remembering, understanding, applying, analyzing, evaluating, and creating. Many instructors not only want their students to remember course content, but also to understand concepts, apply techniques to particular problems, analyze texts and other documents, evaluate competing philosophies, and sometimes create new knowledge.

Although clickers can be effectively used to ask factual recall questions, they can also be used to address learning goals that involve higher-level cognitive processes. Questions that promote these processes are often more challenging to write than factual recall questions, but if course goals involve higher-order thinking skills, then it is worth exploring ways in which clicker questions might be helpful. The examples of clicker questions that follow should provide readers with inspiration for crafting their own clicker questions that emphasize higher-level thinking skills.

Conceptual Understanding Questions

The question in Example 3.2 from the GoodQuestions Project at the Cornell University Department of Mathematics is an example of a conceptual understanding question. It requires students not only to recall the definition of a particular term, the tangent line, but also to understand the concepts associated with that definition. One reason this is an effective question is that the incorrect answer choices are based on common student misconceptions of tangent lines. This question is therefore useful for uncovering and addressing those misconceptions, often a highly productive exercise since students who maintain misconceptions are more likely to struggle with subsequent, more complex course material. Also, determining what students do not understand about a concept and then working to resolve those misunderstandings can be more effective and efficient in promoting student learning than clearly explaining concepts without an understanding of their misconceptions. See the discussion of formative assessment in Chapter Two for an elaboration of this idea.

Example 3.2

What is the equation of the line tangent to the function $f(x) = |x|$ at the point $(0, 0)$?

A. The equation of the tangent line at this point is $y = 0$.

B. There are two tangent lines, with equations $y = -x$ and $y = x$.

C. This function has no tangent line at this point.

D. This function has infinitely many tangent lines at this point.

GoodQuestions Project, Cornell University Department of Mathematics (Terrell, n.d.)

Basing incorrect answer choices on common student misconceptions—drawn from experience with teaching similar students, educational research on student learning, or student responses to free-response questions—is also useful for crafting questions that result in students in a class splitting their vote among multiple answer choices. These distributions of student responses often lead to rich small-group and classwide discussions for the reasons outlined in Chapter One. See Chapter Four for further discussion of ways to craft answer choices based on student misconceptions.

Conceptual understanding questions can be useful for promoting enduring understandings of course material—conceptual understandings that will last far beyond the duration of the course itself (Wiggins & McTighe, 2005). Students can often memorize facts, concepts, and procedures for the short term, then forget them once the test or course is over. Students who fully understand a concept, however, are more likely to retain that understanding later in their academic and vocational careers. Conceptual understanding questions can function as assessments of students' memory or their reading or listening abilities, not their understanding, if not used carefully. When writing a conceptual understanding question, the instructor should ask, "Can my students answer this question successfully without actually understanding the associated concepts?"

Conceptual understanding questions can take the form of classification questions, such as one Philippa Levine asked in her large-enrollment history course at the University of Southern California: "Would you classify Darwin as antislavery, proslavery, or ambivalent on the issue?" Other classification questions might be of the form, "Such-and-such is an example of which of the following concepts?" or "Which of the following is an example of this concept?" Questions phrased in the negative, such as "Which of the following is *not* an example of this concept?" can be more challenging since they often require students to consider more of the answer choices. Questions about characteristics can also be useful, such as, "Which of the following is a characteristic of concept X?" or "The characteristic just described is not possessed by which of the following concepts?"

Other questions focus on explanations for concepts. An instructor might ask, "Which of the following statements best explains concept Y?" and provide students with several explanatory statements, some of which better explain the concept than others. (This type of question should not be confused with a question asking students to explain the causes of a particular concept. Questions asking students to analyze causal relationships are more typically application or critical thinking questions, as described later in the chapter.) One option for generating answer choices for a question like this is to have several students volunteer their explanations for the concept at hand, then have the rest of the students vote on the answer choices thus proposed. Most classroom response systems allow instructors to ask clicker questions that are not planned before class, either verbally or by entering them in the system on the fly. Another option is to have students write their own explanations for the concept, then show them a clicker question with several possible explanations and ask the students to select the explanation that best matches theirs. This format is more challenging for students since it requires them to formulate their own explanation rather than select one from a list.

Conceptual Questions in Quantitative Disciplines. Some types of conceptual understanding questions are particularly useful in the natural sciences, engineering, mathematics, and other disciplines with quantitative elements. For example, Stacy Klein often asks the students in her biomechanics course at Vanderbilt University a conceptual question about a particular topic before having them engage in computational questions on that topic. She has shown her students a diagram of an arm bent at the elbow with a ball in its hand and then asked, "To hold the ball in this position independently, each muscle must provide the same . . . force, torque, or moment arm?" She finds these questions help students understand the big picture of a problem before delving into complex computations.

One useful type of conceptual understanding question is often referred to as a ConcepTest, a term popularized by Harvard physics professor Eric Mazur and used to describe a particular kind of multiple-choice, conceptually oriented question in quantitative disciplines (Mazur, 1997). An example of a ConcepTest is the question in Example 3.3, written by Mazur. Conceptual questions such as this one are useful because they allow instructors to assess their students' understanding of important course concepts independently of their students' computational skills. The question in Example 3.3 could be rewritten as a computational question requiring students to compute the forces involved in hitting the other car and in hitting the wall. Students successfully completing those computations would discover that the correct answer is choice C: the force of impact is the same in either case. However, students who arrived at that answer by computation might not have internalized this fundamental mechanics concept. In fact, Mazur found that students capable of solving computational problems frequently do not understand the concepts in such problems. Since Mazur and many other science instructors who use ConcepTests want students to leave their courses with accurate conceptual understandings of how the world works, these questions are useful ways to determine whether that goal has been met and to focus students' attention during class on important concepts. (As Steven Pollock of the University of Colorado at Boulder physics department points out, the correct physics answer to the question in Example 3.3 is not necessarily the correct ethical answer. Since the force of impact is the same whether one hits the wall or the other car, an argument could be made for hitting the wall to minimize harm to the other driver.)

Example 3.3

Think fast! You've just driven around a curve in a narrow, one-way street at 25 miles per hour when you notice a car identical to yours coming straight toward you at 25 miles per hour. You have only two options: hitting the other car head on or swerving into a massive concrete wall, also head on. In the split second before the impact, you decide to:

A. Hit the other car.

B. Hit the wall.

C. Hit either one—it makes no difference.

Eric Mazur, Physics, Harvard University (Mazur, 1997)

Another type of conceptual question useful in many quantitative fields is what Shane Hutson, Vanderbilt University physics and astronomy professor, calls a ratio reasoning question. These questions ask students to determine the effect of a change in one physical quantity on a related physical quantity. For example, Holly Bender asks students in her veterinary pathology course at Iowa State University whether the concentration of calcium and phosphorous in a cat's bloodstream will increase, decrease, or stay the same given a particular event, such as the removal of a particular organ. Since these concentrations are not independent, she gives her students four answer choices: calcium increases and phosphorous increases, calcium increases and phosphorous decreases, and so on. This question requires her students to understand the essential biophysical relationships of these minerals. Similar ratio reasoning questions can be constructed around almost any mathematical equation that relates real-world quantities. For instance, in a statistics course, an instructor might list several variables that determine the width of a confidence interval and ask the students, "Which of these variables could you increase if you wanted a narrower confidence interval?" Such questions promote intuitive understandings of the relationships conveyed by mathematical equations.

In many quantitative disciplines, mathematical equations constitute only one of several commonly used methods for representing ideas. Often conceptual understanding of the underlying ideas is necessary to translate among various ways of representing those ideas, and so asking students questions that require them to make those translations can be a useful way of assessing their conceptual understanding. The question in Example 3.4 from Barbara Reisner, who teaches chemistry at James Madison University, is an example. It requires students to translate from an equation representing a chemical process to a molecular-level graphical representation of that same process. Similar representation translation questions can be asked in other disciplines. For example, in an economics course, an instructor might display a graph representing the relationship between two quantities and then ask students to select the statement from a list of statements that best describes that relationship.

Example 3.4

Which solution best represents HCl disassociation in solution? (What does the equilibrium picture look like?)

$$HCl_{(aq)} \overset{\longleftarrow}{\longrightarrow} H^+_{(aq)} + Cl^-_{(aq)}$$

A	B	C

Barbara Reisner, Chemistry, James Madison University

APPLICATION QUESTIONS

Application questions require students to apply their knowledge and understanding to particular situations and contexts. For example, Rafael Gely often asks application questions like the one in Example 3.5 in the first-year contracts course he teaches in the University of Cincinnati College of Law. These questions require students to remember and understand various rules and apply them to concrete scenarios. Often the scenarios to which the questions refer are found in the textbook he uses, so students have a chance to read and think about them before class. (This also means he does not need to display these scenarios on-screen in class.) Many of these questions are similar in nature to questions that appear on the nationwide component of the bar exam, which require students to provide accurate reasons for their answers. If only a small minority of students chooses a certain wrong answer on such a clicker question, he does not discuss it, but if a significant percentage of students, perhaps 20 or 30 percent, choose a particular wrong answer, he asks for volunteers to explain their reasoning. He finds that even when students are told that they are wrong, they often still argue their choices vigorously, which he thinks is a useful skill for them to develop as future lawyers. Sometimes he finds their arguments persuasive enough that he awards them credit for their answers.

Example 3.5

Based on the facts of problem 7 [in the students' textbook], in the lawsuit by the student against Mountain Law School, a court will likely find in favor of the:

A. student, if the court finds that the terms of the catalogue are complete, definite, and certain.

B. student, since catalogues are usually considered ads, and ads are always offers.

C. law school, since catalogues can never include all the necessary terms to be deemed definite and complete offers.

D. law school, since the student could not have expected to be taught all the terms included in the catalogue.

Rafael Gely, Law, University of Cincinnati

Application questions are useful for encouraging integrative learning: learning in which students make connections among ideas in a single course, across multiple courses, and across the boundary between academic settings and "the real world." For example, Kristen Hessler often asks application questions in her philosophy courses at the State University of New York at Albany. In the sequence of questions in Example 3.6, she helps students draw connections between their own sense of moral obligations and the utilitarian ethical theory, one of the topics discussed in the course. These questions not only help students relate course content to their personal lives, but they also allow Hessler to assess her students' understanding of course content in the context of a particular application. (Most students choose to help Jim in the first question and save the accident victim in the second question. Choice B is the answer to the third question.)

Example 3.6

Question 1. You promised to meet your friend Jim at 2:00 P.M. to help him with his philosophy homework. At 1:00 P.M., another friend, Sally, calls to ask for your help with her math homework, but you hadn't made any promise to her. You estimate that helping one would produce an equal amount of good as helping the other. Due to other constraints on your time, you can't help both. What should you do?

A. Help Jim.

B. Help Sally.

Question 2. You are on your way to help your friend Jim with his homework, as you promised. On the way, you pass an accident scene. You realize you could save someone's life by pulling the person from a burning car, but that would mean that you would have to break your promise to Jim. What should you do?

A. Save the accident victim and break your promise

B. Help Jim and ignore the accident victim

Question 3. What, according to utilitarianism, accounts for your different intuitions about whether you should keep your promise in the previous two cases?

A. Whether you can consistently will that your maxims be universalized

B. The amount of good produced by keeping your promise compared to the other option in each case

C. The different motives of your actions in each case

D. The existence of different duties of different strengths

Kristen Hessler, Philosophy, State University of New York at Albany

Sometimes students can answer abstract conceptual questions correctly but not perform as well on more concrete questions. For example, Bombaro (2007) describes the use of clickers by academic librarians to facilitate workshops on plagiarism for first-year undergraduate students at Dickinson College. The first few questions in the workshops asked students "to identify definitions of plagiarism," that is, they assessed students' abstract understanding of plagiarism. Later questions "required students to identify plagiarism from samples of plagiaristic writing." Bombaro found that some students who answered the earlier abstract questions correctly subsequently answered the later, application-oriented questions incorrectly.

Instructors sometimes find it difficult to construct answer choices for application questions since they must predict the ways in which students might misapply a concept or procedure to a particular context or problem. (See the discussion of generating answer choices in Chapter Four for some strategies for dealing with this challenge.) Also, if not used carefully, application questions can function as assessments of students' ability to work backward, using the answer choices to deduce the correct answer instead of working through the application as they would if answer choices were not available. As a simple example, a mathematics instructor might ask students, "What value of x solves the equation $4x^2 - 12x + 9 = 0$?" and provide the answer choices 0.5, 1.5, 2, and 3. Instead of factoring the equation, as the instructor might intend students do, students might simply substitute each of the answer choices into the equation to determine the one that solves it. This question, as a result, may not assess the skills it is intended to. One way of compensating for these situations is to have students determine their answers to the question before showing them their answer choices, asking them to select the answer choice that matches their solution.

A variety of types of application questions can be asked with clickers. A question might ask students to view an issue from a particular perspective. These questions might have the form, "What would author X say about situation Y?" or "What would your response to situation Y be if you had the role of Z?" An application question might also ask students to diagnose a particular situation: "Here's a situation. What do you think the problem is?" These questions may have multiple reasonable answers, particularly if the information provided is conflicting or incomplete. Application questions are also useful to ask when discussing case studies with students. (See the discussion of interrupted case studies in Chapter One for an example of this practice.)

Procedural Questions. A common type of application question, particularly in quantitative disciplines, is the procedural question, which requires students to apply knowledge of a procedure or technique to a particular problem or situation. Such questions can focus on the outcome of a procedure or the procedure itself. An example of the former type of question is the one in Example 3.7 from Margaret Logan, who teaches chemistry at the State University of New York at Brockport. Her students find the task of balancing a chemical equation like the one in Example 3.7 challenging. This question provides students with the structure of the equation but asks them to compute the appropriate coefficients for the equation.

Example 3.7

What are the stoichiometric coefficients for the following chemical reaction?

___$NH_3(g)$ + ___$O_2(g)$ → ___$NO(g)$ + ___$H_2O(l)$

A. 2, 5, 2, and 3

B. 3, 6, 3, and 4

C. 4, 5, 4, and 6

D. 5, 5, 5, and 6

Margaret Logan, Chemistry, State University of New York at Brockport

Another example is described by Jenkins (2007), who teaches poetry at Glasgow University in Scotland. She used clickers to teach students metrical analysis of poems. Her example question asks students to predict certain metrical properties of the next line of a given poem. Two of the answer choices in her example question are technically correct, although one demonstrates a fuller understanding of metrical analysis than the other.

Procedural questions can also focus more on a procedure than its outcome, such as the question in Example 3.8 from Adam Lucas, who teaches mathematics at Saint Mary's College of California. Lucas could ask his students to evaluate the integral in the question and select their answers from a list of few possible answer choices. However, by asking the question in the way shown, he focuses students' attention on the substitution procedure used to evaluate these kinds of integrals. The answers students choose reveal which parts of the procedure they do not understand.

Example 3.8

Which of the following is an incorrect step when finding the definite integral $\int_0^4 x^2 \sqrt{1 + x^3}\,dx$ by the substitution method?

A. $u = 1 + x^3$

B. $\dfrac{du}{3} = x^2 dx$

C. $\dfrac{1}{3} \int_1^{65} \sqrt{u}\,du$

D. $\dfrac{1}{3} \int_0^4 \sqrt{u}\,du$

E. None of the above

Adam Lucas, Mathematics, Saint Mary's College of California

Prediction Questions. Often application questions ask students to predict the result of an experiment or procedure. Having students make such predictions and commit to them by submitting them with their clickers can help them become more invested in seeing and understanding the results of an experiment. As a result, prediction questions can help create times for telling, as described in Chapter One, which provides an example of this kind of question that Dennis Jacobs used in his chemistry courses at the University of Notre Dame.

Chemistry and physics instructors often ask prediction questions in advance of classroom demonstrations. Instructors in other disciplines are sometimes able to ask prediction questions as well. Bruce Atwood asks the question in Example 3.9 in his mathematics courses at Beloit College. He shows his students a graphing program that allows him to vary a parameter in a function, such as the parameter ω in the function $\sin(\omega t)$, and asks his students to predict what will happen to the graph of a function when he changes that parameter. After the students vote with their clickers, he demonstrates the correct answer using his graphing program. These prediction questions not only help engage his students in making sense of course material, but similar questions asked after he demonstrates a particular concept in his graphing program allow him to check to see if his program helps students understand that concept.

Example 3.9

How does the plot of $\sin(2t)$ compare to that of $\sin(t)$?

A. It oscillates twice as fast.

B. It oscillates half as fast.

Bruce Atwood, Mathematics, Beloit College

Resa Walch and Amanda Tapler sometimes ask prediction questions in the courses they teach on contemporary issues in wellness at Elon University in North Carolina. For example, they ask their students how many alcoholic drinks they consumed at their last social event. (The fact that students can respond anonymously with their clickers makes it possible to ask such a question.) They also ask their students to predict the outcome of such a question. The differences between the predicted votes and the actual votes are often surprising to students because it turns out that students are not always as risky as they think they are. This activity can lead to a productive classwide discussion of social perceptions of risky behavior and the role that marketing, in particular, plays in those perceptions.

CRITICAL THINKING QUESTIONS

Critical thinking questions operate at the higher levels of Bloom's taxonomy. These questions require students to analyze relationships among multiple concepts or make evaluations based on particular criteria. Elizabeth Cullingford asks challenging critical thinking questions such as the ones in Example 3.10 in the 250-student course she teaches on the masterworks of British literature at the University of Texas at Austin. Many students select answer C in response to the first question in Example 3.10, but those with an understanding of Chaucer's use of irony select answer B. Chaucer uses irony to make that point that as a religious person, the Prioress should be thinking of higher things than charity toward mice. Answer C has some merit, but Cullingford argues that answer B is better. Cullingford also argues that the second question in Example 3.10 has no single best answer. She finds *Hamlet* to be a challenging play in part because what Hamlet is thinking at any point in the play is almost always open to question. Asking this question prompts her students to think critically about each of the suggested answer choices. When she discusses this kind of question with her students after they vote, Cullingford often argues in favor of one of the less popular answer choices as a way to show students the complexity of the question.

Example 3.10

Question 1.

But for to speken of her conscience

She was so charitable and so pitous

She woulde weep if that she saw a mouse

Caught in a trap, if it were dead or bled.

Of smalle houndes had she that she fed

With roasted flesh or milk or wastel bread,

But sore wept she if one of them were dead

Or if men smote it with a yarde, smart;

And all was conscience and tender heart.

—*Canterbury Tales*, Chaucer

Do you think Chaucer's portrait of the Prioress's "conscience" and charity is meant to make us:

A. sympathetic toward her love of animals?

B. critical of her misplaced priorities?

C. aware that women are more tender-hearted than men?

Question 2.

I loved Ophelia. Forty thousand brothers

Could not with all their quantity of love

Make up my sum . . .

Woo't weep? Woo't fight? Woo't fast? Woo't tear thyself?

Woo't drink up eisel? Eat a crocodile?

I'll do't. Dost thou come here to whine?

To outface me with leaping in her grave?

Be buried quick with her and so will I . . .

—*Hamlet*, Act 5, Shakespeare

These lines suggest that:

A. Hamlet really loved Ophelia and is so distraught to learn of her death that he proposes to eat a crocodile.

B. Hamlet thinks that Laertes's grief is mere posturing and mocks it by exaggeration.

C. Hamlet cares little for Ophelia, but is eager to enter into a rhetorical chest-thumping competition with her brother.

Elizabeth Cullingford, English, University of Texas at Austin

When questions calling for critical thinking appear on quizzes and exams, they are often free-response questions, not multiple choice. This is usually because the reasons students give for their answers to these questions are more important than the answers themselves. Instructors are usually interested in the quality and strength of the arguments students make in support of their conclusions and the extent to which those arguments demonstrate ways of knowing or standards of evidence appropriate to the discipline. Instructors are not usually able to make such assessments on the basis of student responses to multiple-choice questions.

As a result, using a multiple-choice question that calls for critical thinking during class requires more than simply having students answer the question using their clickers. Knowing that a certain percentage of students chooses a particular answer does not mean that those students have well-developed and well-reasoned arguments for their answers. Thus, in order to use a critical thinking clicker question during class for assessment purposes, it is often necessary to follow the question with a classwide discussion by which the instructor can hear the reasons students provide for their answers. Otherwise the instructor will know which answers the students choose but not the reasons for those answers.

In contrast to their use on quizzes and exams, questions calling for critical thinking posed during class can be used not only for assessing students but also for engaging students with course material. In fact, multiple-choice critical thinking clicker questions can be used effectively to promote engagement. Having students, in small or large groups, share and analyze each other's arguments for or against answer choices to a critical thinking clicker question can be a productive way to help them practice and develop their critical thinking skills. Although instructors can be successful in promoting these kinds of discussions in response to open-ended critical thinking questions during class without clickers, a classroom response system allows an instructor to ask every student to respond to a question posed, which encourages more students to engage with the question. Furthermore, the simple act of pushing a button to commit to an answer can encourage students to engage more seriously. For example, Robert Bartsch has his students review journal articles in his psychology courses at the University of Houston at Clear Lake and then vote on the construct validity of the research as high, medium, or low. There is often a diversity of opinions, so he has students defend their answers during a classwide discussion and then vote again.

Use of a classroom response system also allows an instructor to assess the thinking of an entire class of students, not just the thinking of the students who are willing to speak up and participate in a classwide discussion. Instructors can find it productive to ask a challenging critical thinking question, have students discuss the question in small groups and respond using clickers, and then use the results of the clicker question to launch a classwide discussion.

Given the typical complexity of critical thinking questions, it can be important to prevent students from oversimplifying such a question presented in a multiple-choice format. For instance, some students might assume that because they answer a critical thinking question correctly, they have a full understanding of the question. Since accurate arguments for or against an answer choice are typically complex and sophisticated, such students may overestimate their understanding of the question. Thus, it can be important to spend class time discussing these questions with students and emphasizing that the reasons they provide for their answers and the quality of their thinking are more important than the answers themselves.

Another approach to focusing students' attention on the reasons for and against various responses is to follow a critical thinking clicker question with a reason-focused question asking each student to identify from a list the reason he or she answered the first question the way that he or she did. This provides the instructor a better sense of the thinking of the entire class, helping to compensate for the limitations of using critical thinking questions for assessment purposes, and can serve as a foundation for an energetic classwide discussion. Example 3.11 features such a reason-focused question asked by Barbara Reisner, who teaches chemistry at James Madison University.

Example 3.11

Reaction rates increase as the temperature of a reaction increases. Identify any statements that can be used to explain this phenomenon:

I. Molecules collide more frequently at higher temperatures.

II. More molecules have sufficient energy to react.

III. More molecules collide with the correct orientation.

A. I only

B. II only

C. I and II

D. II and III

E. I, II, and III

Barbara Reisner, Chemistry, James Madison University

This use of a reason-focused question works better for some critical thinking questions than others. If the second question is planned before class, it must feature a fairly comprehensive list of reasons students might give for any of the answers to the first question, unless the instructor can accurately predict the results of the first question. In that case, the second question need only list reasons students might provide for the single predicted response to the first question. Another option is to construct the second question on the fly after the first question, asking a few students to volunteer reasons for their answers to the first question, then asking all students to choose from among these reasons. If the first question has a single popular or correct answer, this process is a little easier, since the second question, constructed on the fly, can focus on reasons for that single answer.

One-Best-Answer Questions. Another distinction between multiple-choice questions used on quizzes and exams and those used during a class session, particularly those that call for critical thinking, is that multiple-choice questions used during a class session need not have single correct answers. For example, Stuart Beatty often asks one-best-answer questions in his courses at the Ohio State University College of Pharmacy. The questions in Example 3.12 explore the multiple ways a pharmacist might treat a patient, some of which are often better than others depending on the information available in a particular case. Beatty asks his students to make decisions about the best treatment plans in the context of particular patients.

Example 3.12

Question 1. RR is a 22-year-old Mexican American newly diagnosed with type 1 diabetes. He weighs 68 kg. You need to start him on an insulin regimen. He has no insurance, did not complete high school, and speaks limited English. What is the best insulin regimen to start him on?

A. Glargine 15 units at bedtime plus sliding-scale lispro with meals

B. NPH 30 units twice daily

C. Mixed insulin 70/30, 20 units in the morning and 10 units at bedtime

D. Glargine 15 units at bedtime and lispro 5 units with meals

E. Levemir 15 units twice daily

Question 2. Two weeks later, RR comes in for follow-up. He brings his SMBG log book, and you see that most of his prebreakfast numbers have been high—around 200. After questioning RR, he says he has been waking in the middle of the night with a lot of sweating. The most likely reason for his high AM sugars is:

A. Dawn phenomenon

B. Poor dinner choices

C. Not enough insulin in the evening

D. Somogyi effect

E. Incorrect use of BG meter

Stuart Beatty, Pharmacy, Ohio State University

Ron McClamrock also asks one-best-answer questions in his philosophy courses at the State University of New York at Albany. His question in Example 3.13 asks students to choose the best answer from among several defensible ones.

Example 3.13

We've looked at three problems for interactive dualism: the unintelligibility of interaction, Occam's razor/explanatory simplicity, and the mental effects of physical trauma. Which do you think best succeeds in giving at least some decent reason to worry about the dualist view?

A. Unintelligibility of interaction

B. Occam's razor/explanatory simplicity

C. Mental effects of physical trauma

D. None is best, but at least two are some reason to worry

E. None is any reason to worry about dualism at all

Ron McClamrock, Philosophy, State University of New York at Albany

Francisco Estrada-Belli sometimes takes a different approach to one-best-answer questions in his introduction to anthropology course at Vanderbilt University. On the first day of class, he poses the question, "What is a civilization?" He then has several students volunteer definitions for the term *civilization*. He writes these on the chalkboard and sometimes adds one or two alternate definitions of his own. He then has his students use their clickers to vote on the best definition. This prompts the students to consider the various features of each of the proposed definitions and interests them in finding out the correct answer. After the vote, he leads a classwide discussion about the question, surfacing the various reasons students have for their choices. It is all a bit of a trick, however, since anthropologists do not agree on the definition of the term, which is one of the points Estrada-Belli makes in this first class session. He lets his students know that they will continue to explore this multifaceted question throughout the semester.

Typically a multiple-choice quiz or exam question needs to have a single correct answer so that it can be used to evaluate student learning. Since in-class clicker questions are often used more for engaging students than assessing them, these questions need not have single correct answers. Asking critical thinking questions with multiple correct answers, some of which may be more or less reasonable under certain conditions and according to different ways of knowing or standards of evidence, can be a very effective way to engage students in thoughtful and reflective discussions. Although these questions can be posed in ways to allow each student to select multiple answers at once, these questions are often best posed as one-best-answer questions (Case & Swanson, 2002) that require each student to select the one choice he or she thinks best answers the question at hand. This kind of question requires students not only to analyze a particular situation or set of issues but also to evaluate possible responses, making decisions about their relative merits. Such questions can lead to productive discussions of the criteria by which these kinds of decisions are made.

Perry (1999) and others, including Belenky, Clinchy, Goldberger, and Tarule (1986), have shown that many students come to college believing that every question, problem, or challenge has a single right answer. This dualistic thinking can lead students to find one-best-answer questions challenging and disconcerting. These questions can help students move beyond this kind of thinking since they demonstrate to students that not every question is as black-and-white as they would like to believe.

In Perry's model of the intellectual development of college students, those who move away from such dualistic thinking often move to the other extreme, coming to believe that there are no right answers, that everything is just opinion. Provided that some attention is paid during class to the reasons for various answer choices, one-best-answer questions and other critical thinking questions can help show these students that some answers are indeed better than others, that opinions should be supported with arguments, and that criteria and standards of evidence can be used to evaluate those arguments. These questions can help students start to see that an answer to a tough question depends on one's perspective and the criteria one uses to evaluate options. Although one-best-answer questions can help students develop their thinking in the ways described here, the process is difficult, and instructors asking these kinds of clicker questions can find that students resist this process.

Anthony Crider of Elon University in North Carolina asks the same clicker question repeatedly to assess his students as they grapple with the role of evidence in his thirty-student astronomy courses. He asks, "Do you think that United States astronauts landed on the moon?" at the beginning of a unit on the moon landing. At this point, most of his students answer affirmatively, so he shows them a documentary arguing that the moon landing was a hoax. Crider finds that the documentary is well produced but relies on the testimony of nonexperts to make its case. He asks the same clicker question again after they see the documentary and sometimes has up to half of his students vote no, having been convinced by the documentary. He then spends a few class periods exploring the issue with his students using *National Geographic* video clips designed to rebut the documentary, as well as other, more lighthearted video clips exploring the topic. He polls his students periodically during this process, asking them the same question. Crider does not want to move on to the next topic until his students are convinced that the moon landing was not a hoax, and the clickers provide the data he needs to make this decision. The fact that the students respond anonymously is very important, since a show of hands typically does not reveal the students who believe that the moon landing was a hoax.

Peer Assessment. Some instructors have students assess each other's presentations, papers, or other work during class with clickers.

This not only provides students with potentially valuable feedback on their work, but also helps students better understand the criteria by which quality is judged in a particular course or discipline. Meagan Bowler, a librarian at Mount Royal College, often leads information literacy sessions for students. In some of these sessions, she has students work in small groups of four to six to assess the scholarly quality of Web resources. Each group reports its assessments to the entire class, identifying each Web resource as appropriate for use in an academic paper or not. Then the other students respond to a clicker question: "Do you agree with this assessment—yes or no?" When there is significant disagreement, Bowler leads a classwide discussion about the resource, giving students a chance to ask questions of the presenting students. Bowler finds that displaying the results of the clicker questions to the class encourages students to speak up and question the presenting students, since students who disagree with the presenting students can know from the clicker question results that they are not alone in thinking so. The classwide discussions help the students better understand the criteria by which a resource is judged scholarly.

Kori Street, also at Mount Royal College, includes a couple of problem-based learning activities (Duch, Gron, & Allen, 2001) in her nonmajors history courses, activities in which students tackle complex problems that require them to practice thinking, reasoning, and usually debating like historians and to critically evaluate issues from multiple perspectives. In one such activity, Street assigns to each group a different film about the Holocaust. Each group's task is to evaluate their film for use in a public presentation about the Holocaust and to "defend" the film to their peers as historically meaningful. Their peers evaluate each group's presentation using clicker questions based on a rubric Street designed for this purpose. The rubric consists of descriptions of multiple levels of quality (poor, acceptable, good, excellent) in several categories. Students respond to a clicker question for each category asking them to evaluate their peers' presentation according to the levels of quality given in the rubric for that category. After each clicker question, the results are shared with the class, and the presenting students are given a chance to defend their presentation to the class. Then the students revote, evaluating the presenting students in the same category but factoring in the additional comments of the presenting students.

Street finds that this system keeps the presenting students from feeling attacked by other students or their instructor but also motivates them to defend themselves. The public criticism students receive during these activities can potentially be harsh, but since students are given the chance to defend themselves, most take the criticism well. There can be some defensiveness, but no more than would be present without the clickers. As a result, Street finds her peer assessment activities effective at promoting useful classwide discussions and debates, even among nonmajors. The peer assessment also improves student performance on these tasks. Street finds that students sometimes feel as if they can slack off a little when reporting to their instructor, the expert, but knowing their peers will be evaluating them encourages them to take the tasks more seriously.

Street finds her students participate fully in these activities. Peer pressure keeps them from just giving each other all A's. Also, she asks students to defend their assessments of their peers, so they must answer the peer assessment clicker questions carefully. On occasion, students give positive evaluations to a group with a great presentation but poor content. Street intervenes in these situations, saying something like, "That's not where I'm leaning in evaluating this argument. Can anyone say why I might be leaning that way?" This helps to keep the discussion focused on critical thinking.

Free-Response Questions

Some classroom response systems allow students to respond to open-ended, free-response questions by submitting a number, a word or phrase, or even a sentence. Instructors can find asking these questions useful when they are not sure how students will respond to a question, making the construction of answer choices difficult. A question with a very large set of possible responses might be asked as a free-response question as well. Asking a multiple-choice question with fifty answer choices is not practical, for instance. Free-response questions are also useful for assessing students' ability to create, generate, or produce something. As noted above, creating is one of the six basic cognitive processes in learning according to Bloom's taxonomy (Anderson & Krathwohl, 2001), and it is a process that can be very difficult, if not impossible, to develop and assess through multiple-choice questions. For example, often the first step in solving a complex problem is to brainstorm ideas that might be helpful in solving it. Having students brainstorm at the beginning of a class session or unit dealing with a challenging problem can be an important step in the learning process, but multiple-choice clicker questions cannot be used to have students submit their ideas. Free-response questions can be useful in support of this kind of brainstorming.

Of the various types of free-response questions, numerical answer questions are perhaps used most frequently, particularly in quantitative disciplines. For example, Matthew Mulvaney uses numerical answer questions in the statistics course he teaches in the Department of Psychology at the State University of New York at Brockport. He teaches a five-step procedure for conducting hypothesis tests, first working through an example for his students, then having his students apply the process to a second example. Students work through this example in groups, answering free-response numerical answer questions along the way. Mulvaney's classroom response system displays a histogram of responses, scaled to a number line with bins created automatically. This enables him to quickly make sense of the students' responses to numerical answer questions. If there is confusion among his students on these clicker questions, Mulvaney walks them through the calculation. The numerical answer clicker questions help to make sure his students do not get too lost during these lengthy problems.

Logistically, free-response questions can be challenging to use for two reasons. One is that students need some kind of input device that allows more than multiple-choice answer input—a clicker with an LCD screen and an alphanumerical entry mode, a laptop running an application that functions as part of a classroom response system, or a cell phone with text-messaging or wireless Internet functionality. The second challenge is the display of results of these questions. Answers to multiple-choice questions are simple to aggregate and analyze with bar charts. Answers to free-response questions require more sophisticated aggregation and analysis tools. More work on the instructor's part is often needed to make sense of answers to free-response questions. As a result, these questions can sometimes take more time than is possible.

As of this writing, free-response questions are not frequently used with classroom response systems due to the technological limitations of most such systems and the fact that multiple-choice questions are much simpler to use for assessment or engagement purposes. As classroom response system technology becomes more sophisticated, allowing faster and easier student input of responses as well as faster and easier analysis of student responses by instructors, it is likely that more instructors will make use of free-response questions in the ways described here. (See the discussion of higher-tech classroom response system options in Chapter Five for additional thoughts on where the technology might be headed.)

Process Questions

Process questions are used to gather information from students helpful in shaping how they interact with each other during class and with course material. These questions include those that request student opinions and experiences, ask students to assess their confidence in answering content questions, monitor the ways in which students engage in course activities, and collect data from students used in classroom experiments.

Student Perspective Questions

An instructor can ask students a variety of clicker questions that are not designed to assess their learning but to surface their perspectives instead. Demographic questions ask students to report various personal characteristics: their age, gender, the region of the country in which they grew up, religious preferences, political preferences, or whether they have taken a particular prerequisite course, for instance. Opinion questions ask students to share their opinions, feelings, and beliefs about topics or issues relevant to the course. Personal experience questions ask students to share aspects of their own experience—activities in which they have engaged, people with whom they have associated, places they have visited.

Student perspective questions can be used to help instructors get to know their students. Each class of students is unique, and it is often important for instructors not to rely on assumptions about students, their opinions, and their experiences. Asking these questions can provide useful information about students that helps prevent instructors from making unfounded assumptions about them and helps instructors tailor learning experiences to the unique makeup of students engaged in those learning experiences.

For example, Philippa Levine uses opinion questions to learn about the students in her course, The Evolution Debates, at the University of Southern California. Given the topic of the course, she sometimes finds it surprisingly easy to say something that seems harmless to her but off-putting to some of her students. By knowing where her students stand on sensitive topics, she is better able to avoid this. The question in Example 3.14, for instance, provides insight into her students' religious beliefs. She finds that her students think it important that an instructor respect the beliefs of students. By asking questions such as this, she is demonstrating that respect, and her students respond positively. The ability to answer anonymously is an important ingredient here.

Example 3.14

Which of the following statements most closely matches what you think?

A. Humans evolved from other life forms with divine assistance.

B. Humans evolved from other life forms without divine assistance.

C. Humans were created directly by a divine being within the past 10,000 years.

Philippa Levine, History, University of Southern California

Rafael Gely teaches a one-week introductory course for incoming law students at the University of Cincinnati. He uses clickers to collect demographic information from his students, including where they went to school, how long they have been out of school, their political views, and their judicial views. He finds that often students at this stage of their law education are not entirely sure how to describe their judicial views. After the week-long course in which they learn more about the judicial landscape, Gely asks them again to express their judicial views using clickers to see how they have changed their understanding of their own views.

Student perspective questions can also be used to help students in a class get to know each other. Just as instructors can rely on unfounded assumptions about the makeup of students in a class, students can do so as well. Polling students about their opinions and experiences, and then sharing those results with the class, can help students get a better idea of who their peers are. This can help students engage in small-group and classwide discussions that are more respectful and founded on a better understanding of the participants of those discussions. Furthermore, showing students the variety of characteristics, opinions, and experiences represented by their peers can help them see the value in considering perspectives other than their own. When students learn, for instance, that 30 percent of their peers disagree with them on some issue, they might be more likely to engage in a serious discussion of that topic, thinking more deeply about their own reasons for their opinions and listening more attentively to the reasons others give for different views. This use of demographic, opinion, and personal experience questions is enhanced by the ability of a classroom response system to display results of a question to an entire class immediately after students have responded to the question, since students need to see the class results in order to benefit from these questions in these ways.

Corly Brooke uses opinion questions in her two-hundred-student human development course at Iowa State University in part to help her students realize that their peers have a variety of opinions on important issues. She finds questions that ask students to make particular decisions that reflect their opinions and values most effective. For example, she asks students whether they would bank their child's umbilical cord blood if it cost a certain dollar amount. She also asks decision-oriented questions that require students to take on unfamiliar roles. For instance, she asks students, "Which of the following courses of action would you be likely to take if your daughter told you she was in a physically abusive intimate relationship?" She finds helpful questions that are concrete and true-to-life. This type of question is effective at generating small-group discussions. The results of these questions show her students the variety of opinions people hold regarding these topics, and the process of asking students to respond to these questions helps them think more deeply about their own opinions and prepares them to make future life decisions. Sometimes she asks the same question before and after a unit and notes that showing her students the results of these questions can help them see what they have learned.

Student perspective questions can also help students see the relevance of course content to their own lives by demonstrating how many of their peers are affected by topics covered in a course. It is one thing to read in a textbook that, for instance, 20 percent of Americans have dealt with a particular hardship. It is another thing entirely to find out that 20 percent of one's peers have dealt with that hardship. In the latter case, students are more likely to see the value in discussing how people deal with that hardship since they know it affects someone they know. This is another use that benefits from a classroom response system's ability to share results of such questions with an entire class. Similarly, these questions can help students see the relevance of course content to their own lives by encouraging them to recall and reflect on personal experiences that connect with course topics. Asking a student to remember a time when he or she engaged in some kind of activity prior to a more theoretical or academic discussion of that kind of activity helps prepare the student to value and engage in that discussion. For this use, it is helpful when every student in a class reflects on such a question. Classroom response systems can encourage this by making it possible for each student to submit an answer to the question.

Resa Walch and Amanda Tapler teach a course on contemporary issues in wellness at Elon University. They take advantage of the anonymity provided by their classroom response systems to ask questions that help students connect their own experiences to course material. For example, they ask students whether they have close family members who deal with alcoholism. Many students do, so the results of this question make an effective segue into a discussion of biological risk factors for alcoholism. Another question they ask in the same unit is, "Have you ended an evening early to care for a drunk friend?'' They ask similar personal experience questions about sleep, another topic in the course, such as, "How many hours of sleep do you usually get?" "How many hours of sleep do you need to perform optimally?" "Why don't you get enough sleep?"

Walch and Tapler say that these kinds of questions, particularly when asked at the beginning of a class session or unit, make the course material relevant to the students in a way that the sharing of generic research findings does not. Students who are sometimes hesitant to believe national data on a particular issue, for instance, are more convinced when data collected from their peers during class match those data. In fact, Walch and Tapler find that students believe information about their own personal experiences more when it is collected during class with clickers than when it is collected using pencil-and-paper forms and collated between classes. They know that the clicker data have not been tweaked by the instructors to fit the instructors' agenda.

Opinion and personal experience questions can also be useful in generating small-group and classwide discussion in much the same way that application and critical thinking questions can. Having students share reasons for their opinions or provide details about their personal experiences can be a productive way to engage them in discussion. Often these discussions, based on the students' experiences, can help prepare students to engage in more scholarly discussions of course material. For example, an instructor might ask an opinion question that opens the door to a discussion of disciplinary methods of inquiry that students can use to generate evidence in favor of their initial opinions. In addition, students who find out that some of their peers agree with them on a particular issue might be more likely to speak up and participate in a classwide discussion of that issue. This can encourage students who hold minority perspectives by showing them that they are not alone in those ideas.

Opinion and personal experience questions can also help instructors engage in the kinds of agile teaching described in Chapter Two. If most students answer an opinion question, for example, in one of two ways, an instructor might respond by focusing subsequent classwide discussion or lecture on explorations of those two opinions. It might be even more productive to spend some time on the opinions not well represented among the students in order to help students consider perspectives other than their own. The instructor might play the devil's advocate role here, helping students to understand why others might approach the question from certain perspectives. Asking such a question using clickers means that the instructor receives information on the distribution of student opinions, information that can be used to determine useful follow-up interactions.

Often the success of these kinds of questions depends on the ability of students to respond anonymously. Clickers allow an instructor to collect responses to such questions in such a way that students are not aware of the individual answers of their peers. They see the class results only in the aggregate. This makes it safer for students to answer questions honestly. One can imagine it might be difficult for students who see themselves in the minority on a particular issue to raise their hands and share their thoughts on that issue with the class. (Some students would relish the opportunity to challenge the views of their peers, of course, but many students are hesitant to appear different to their peers.) Asking these questions with clickers allows students to share their thoughts and experiences in ways that do not identify them.

Bear in mind, however, that classroom response systems can usually be configured so that student responses are not anonymous to their instructors. Some students may be hesitant to share their perspectives honestly if they feel that their instructor is "watching" them through their clicker responses, particularly if they believe that their grades will suffer if their opinions do not match those of their instructors. Depending on the question and the students, it may be important for some instructors to use their classroom response systems in true anonymous modes, in which students are not identified in the systems at all.

Another challenge when asking student perspective questions centers on how instructors respond to minority opinions and perspectives expressed through these questions. This challenge can occur when a student's expectation of the results of a student perspective question does not match the actual results. For instance, some students might expect to find themselves in the majority of student opinion on a certain issue. If the results of a clicker question on that issue reveal that these students are in the minority, they might be discouraged from contributing to a class-wide discussion on the issue. Other students can be discouraged when they expect themselves to be in the minority on an issue but are surprised at just how few of their peers agree with them. Instructors in these situations might need to take care in how they facilitate a discussion of such minority views. They may need to speak on behalf of students who might possess minority views if the students are not willing to speak for themselves. They might also ask students in the majority to imagine themselves in the minority and share reasons that they might possess those minority perspectives. It can be useful to step back and engage students in a discussion about ways in which the class can discuss certain topics that respect minority views. If students in the majority are more respectful, students in the minority may be more likely to participate in such discussions. Instructors may find it useful to review the results of a student perspective clicker questions without showing those results to students before deciding how to proceed with a classwide discussion of the question.

Confidence Level Questions

Imagine asking students a true-or-false question. Suppose that 70 percent of the students answer the question correctly. This could indicate that 70 percent of the students fully understand the question. But it could also mean that only 20 or 30 percent of the students do, the rest having answered correctly by guessing randomly among the two answer choices. Knowing how many students guessed would be important in making subsequent teaching decisions. In cases like this, it can be helpful to ask students how confident they are in their answers. Imagine following the true-false question with a second question: "How confident are you in your answer to the previous question?" with answer choices "very confident," "somewhat confident," and "not at all confident." Results of this second question would be helpful in interpreting the results of the first one.

Dennis Jacobs asks these kinds of confidence questions in the chemistry courses he teaches at the University of Notre Dame. After a content question, he often has students indicate their confidence—high, medium, or low—in their answers. This motivates them to think about and weigh arguments that might compete with the ones they use to answer his questions. Since Jacobs often has students respond to clicker questions twice, once individually and once again after small-group or classwide discussion, students are given the opportunity to reflect on their own learning. For instance, a student whose first vote was correct might reflect, "I was correct. Why didn't I say I was highly confident? Because I couldn't defend my reasoning." This metacognitive reflection can play an important role in helping students improve their learning process.

Students in Jacobs's course score points based on the accuracy of their answers and their confidence (see Table 3.1). He finds that students understand this scoring system fairly quickly and that it encourages them to rate their confidence accurately. It is in their best interest to do so, since they can earn extra credit from these questions. Since many of Jacobs's questions are used to generate times for telling, as described in Chapter One, his students find the questions challenging. Since students frequently answer the questions incorrectly, he assigns only extra credit for these questions. Regular credit questions would raise the stakes too high and change the spirit of the class.

Another way to ask a confidence-level question is to ask students how confident they are that they could answer a particular content question, respond well to a particular essay question, or solve a particular problem were they asked to do so. Asking students to assess their confidence in approaching a task that they have not actually completed is perhaps not as useful as asking them to assess their confidence in an answer to a question to which they have already responded. However, this kind of question can be asked of more than just multiple-choice questions. For instance, an

TABLE 3.1. CONFIDENCE QUESTION GRADING SYSTEM.

Confidence Level	Correct Answer	Incorrect Answer
High	5 points	0 points
Medium	4 points	1 point
Low	3 points	2 points

Source: Dennis Jacobs, Chemistry, University of Notre Dame.

instructor might ask students to rate their confidence in writing an essay on a particular topic or in designing a particular kind of circuit in an engineering class. These predictive confidence questions also take less time for students to answer since they do not require them to complete a task before answering. These kinds of confidence-level questions can be useful in determining tasks for which students need assistance and can work very well at the start of a session designed to prepare students for an exam. (See the discussion of background knowledge probes in Chapter Two for an example of these kinds of confidence questions from Thomas Palmeri of the Vanderbilt University Department of Psychology.) These questions are also similar to those that appear in the knowledge surveys described by Nuhfer (2003).

Both types of confidence-level questions provide instructors with a level of information about their students' learning beyond a simple assessment of their accuracy in answering a clicker question. Moreover, the questions can help students become better learners by asking them to assess their own learning. This type of reflection—What do I know? What don't I know? What do I know, but not that well?—is called *metacognition* and is an important component of how experts in a field learn (Bransford, Brown, & Cocking, 2000). Providing opportunities for students to practice this type of reflection can help them develop expert habits of mind.

Some classroom response systems allow the results of two questions to be combined in a single bar chart. Figure 3.1 provides an example of how responses from a content question followed by a confidence-level question could be combined in a useful manner. This figure makes it clear that many of the students who selected answer B lacked confidence in their answers, while most of those who selected answer C were highly confident. Some classroom response systems may even enable students to submit their confidence level along with their answer to a content question, making it even easier to ask confidence level questions.

It is worth noting that a fairly simple way to assess students' confidence in their answers to content questions is to include an "I don't know" option as an answer choice. This does not provide the same quality of information about student learning as the methods described do, but it does allow students who are truly

FIGURE 3.1.   STACKED BAR CHART SHOWING HOW CONFIDENT STUDENTS ARE IN
THEIR ANSWERS TO A CONTENT QUESTION.

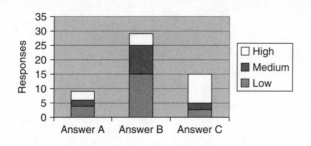

confused about a question a way to express that confusion other than guessing randomly. (See Chapter Four for more on the "I don't know" option.)

MONITORING QUESTIONS

Classroom response systems can also be used to monitor various aspects of the student learning experience beyond comprehension and confidence levels. For example, if students in a course are required to complete a semester-long assignment such as a paper, project, or presentation, an instructor might ask them to report using clickers how much progress they have made at various times during the semester. This gives the instructor a sense of where students are in the assignment, which can be useful in planning ways to support students as they work. It also gives the instructor an opportunity to tell students how much progress they should have completed by that point, giving a benchmark by which they can compare their progress. Angel Hoekstra, for instance, uses assignment monitoring questions such as, "Have you written the first draft of your paper?" in the sociology course she teaches at the University of Colorado at Boulder. She finds these questions useful for starting class discussions about study habits and for prompting procrastinating students to begin their assignments.

Similarly, it can be helpful to ask students after the first or second assignment of the semester (a problem set, a short paper, a lab report) how long it took them to complete that assignment.

This provides a sense of how difficult the assignment was for the student, useful information to have when planning future assignments. It also allows students to compare themselves to their peers. If the average response is three hours, a student who took five hours to complete the assignment might be encouraged to seek extra help in the course. And if the average response is three hours, a student who finished the assignment in an hour but performed poorly on it might be encouraged to spend more time on subsequent assignments.

Another type of monitoring question addresses the common criticism that students read a course syllabus on the first day of class, then seem to forget what it said. An instructor might quiz students on various points made in the course syllabus throughout the semester in order to remind students of those points. For example, an instructor might ask students how many problem set grades they are allowed to drop in a course. Many students would likely recall that particular course policy, but some might forget it over time. This clicker question can be a reminder.

An instructor might also ask students prior to the first exam which of a set of possible study strategies is likely to be most effective in preparing for the exam. Results from this clicker question provide a picture of students' study habits and an opportunity to discuss effective study skills. I experimented with this technique in a statistics course. I asked a few students to volunteer their preferred exam preparation strategies. These were typed in a clicker question, and the students voted on their favorite study strategy. Fifty-eight percent voted for "redo homework problems." This is a relatively poor study strategy in my opinion since students can be fooled by the familiarity of old homework problems into thinking they understand the course material better than they actually do. Not a single student suggested a much better study strategy: work through homework problems that were not assigned originally and check the answers. Asking this clicker question gave me a chance to discuss this more effective strategy.

Yet another type of monitoring question takes the kinds of questions that frequently appear on end-of-semester course evaluation forms that students complete and asks them during the semester. Asking students questions such as, "How well are you able to follow lectures in this course?" "How challenging is the out-of-class work in this course compared to work in your other courses?'' and "How helpful is the instructor outside class?'' as clicker questions during the semester, whether or not the results are shared with students, can provide instructors with useful feedback on the learning experience. Instructors routinely act on this kind of feedback after a course has ended. However, gathering it during the semester allows them to respond in ways that improve the experience for them and for their students.

Corly Brooke used clickers to gather feedback on her teaching in her human development course at Iowa State University. In response to an open-ended question on a midterm feedback form, some students indicated they were not happy with Brooke's inclusion of her personal experiences during lecture. She asked all of her students what they thought about this approach using the clickers, and almost all were in favor of it. Without the clickers, she might have gone along with what turned out to be a minority opinion.

A makeshift classroom response system provided Charlene Harkins with useful feedback about her large-enrollment nutrition course at the University of Minnesota at Duluth one semester. She had noticed that each day in a prior semester, ten or twelve students would e-mail or text-message questions to her e-mail account during class. Harkins thought there might be a way to respond to these questions during class when they were on the minds of students instead of later in the day. She posted her cell phone number at the start of class and encouraged her students to text her questions during class. Students text-messaged questions to her cell phone during class, but she quickly found that she could not monitor those questions and deliver her lecture at the same time. She then posted her teaching assistant's cell phone number (with her permission), and the teaching assistant acted as an aggregator for the student questions. As important questions were text-messaged to the assistant during class, she would raise her hand and report them to Harkins.

Harkins found that this system worked very well. She found that there was a group of students who were not willing to share their questions publicly during class, either because of peer pressure to appear knowledgeable or because they were not willing to share questions about their personal experiences publicly, but were willing to text-message those questions to her teaching assistant. On a couple of occasions, students text-messaged questions about their personal experiences to the assistant (for example, questions about their mothers and osteoporosis), and when the teaching assistant publicly shared these questions, deidentified to protect the students' privacy, the course content became more relevant for all the students. One disadvantage of this system was that all of Harkins's students had her teaching assistant's phone number and ended up calling or text-messaging the assistant too often outside class.

Harkins's text-messaging system is an example of what is often called a *backchannel*, a system by which students in a class session or audience members in a presentation can communicate with the instructor or presenter or even with each other. Harkins's backchannel system was a free-response version of the simpler backchannel system described in Chapter Two. As classroom response system technology advances, more systems will likely be able to facilitate various kinds of backchannels. (See the discussion of higher-tech systems in Chapter Five for more on this topic.)

CLASSROOM EXPERIMENTS

A final set of process-oriented clicker questions are ones used to facilitate classroom experiments often used in social science classrooms. For example, Bill Hill uses clickers to facilitate experiments and demonstrations in his psychology courses at Kennesaw State University. He says that many psychology textbooks describe these classroom activities, and he needs spend only a little effort in adapting them for use with clickers. For instance, he sometimes shows his students a list of words for a brief time, then takes away the word list and asks them to write down as many of the words they can remember. He then takes several words in sequence and asks his students to report using their clickers whether they remembered each of the words. The students' responses illustrate several important concepts in the study of memory, including the primacy effect, in which words at the beginning of the list are remembered more frequently; the recency effect, in which words at the end of the list are also remembered more frequently but not as frequently as those at the start of the list; and the fact that distinctive words in the middle of the list are remembered more frequently than other middle words. Hill also uses this experiment to illustrate the false memory effect. This occurs when all the words on the list are related to a word not on the list, such as *needle*. Although the word *needle* is not on the list, 30 to 40 percent of students claim to remember seeing it. Hill finds that having his students experience experiments such as these leads to greater student engagement. Prior to his use of clickers, he had students fill out written surveys, collated them after class, and presented the data to his students in the next class. Not only do clickers save a lot of his time, but he also suspects some benefit to seeing immediate results in these kinds of experiments. Cleary (2008) also describes the use of clickers in psychology courses to demonstrate behavioral research findings.

I used the clicker question in Example 3.15 in a statistics course to illustrate the conjunction fallacy—the idea described by Tversky and Kahneman (1982) that people will choose a more descriptive scenario as more likely than a less descriptive scenario even when the rules of probability would indicate they should not. Although reasonable people might disagree on the relative likelihood of the man Bill described in the question being an accountant or playing jazz for a hobby, it can be said with certainty that the probability of Bill being an accountant who plays jazz is smaller than the probability that Bill plays jazz. The former event is a subset of the latter. However, 61 percent of my students selected choice 2 in spite of its impossibility. (The remaining 39 percent selected choice 1, which is possible.) The results of this question served to illustrate to students how common it is for people to fall victim to the conjunction fallacy. They also created a time for telling about the tools from probability that explain the impossibility of choice 2. Once the students were shown the appropriate Venn diagram, the impossibility was clear to them.

Example 3.15

Bill is 34 years old. He is intelligent but unimaginative, compulsive, and generally lifeless. In school, he was strong in mathematics but weak in social studies and humanities. Rank the following statements in order of decreasing likelihood.

Bill is a physician who plays poker for a hobby.

Bill is an architect.

Bill is an accountant.

Bill plays jazz for a hobby.

Bill surfs for a hobby.

Bill is a reporter.

Bill is an accountant who plays jazz for a hobby.

Bill climbs mountains for a hobby.

Let A = "Bill is an accountant," J = "Bill plays jazz for a hobby," and AJ = "Bill is an accountant who plays jazz for a hobby." Which of the following describes your ranking of these statements, where > means "more likely than"?

1. A > J > AJ

2. A > AJ > J

3. J > A > AJ

4. J > AJ > A

5. AJ > A > J

6. AJ > J > A

Derek Bruff, Mathematics, Vanderbilt University, based on Tversky and Kahneman (1982)

See Hinde and Hunt (2006) for an example of a classroom experiment in an economics course that used clickers to help students understand the Prisoner's Dilemma. Cheung (2008) describes a cell-phone-based classroom response system used to facilitate "the ultimatum game" in another economics course.

CHAPTER FOUR

TEACHING CHOICES

This chapter explores a variety of frequently asked pedagogical questions about teaching with classroom response systems. Since the answers to many of these questions depend on teaching goals and context, the discussion focuses on examining the advantages and disadvantages of various choices.

USE OF CLASS TIME

Given that having students respond to and discuss clicker questions takes class time, do instructors using clickers find it difficult to include as much content in their courses as they would without clickers?

Instructors have a variety of reactions to the challenge of making class time available for interactive clicker questions. Some instructors find it difficult to include as much content in their courses when they begin using clickers but are satisfied with the trade-off. They often believe that if students' misconceptions are not addressed, subsequent course material will not make sense to students, so class time spent resolving those misconceptions through clicker questions is well spent. Adam List, who teaches chemistry at Vanderbilt University, notes that a useful conceptual question might take ten minutes of class time. He sometimes finds it challenging to make this time available, particularly since he teaches in a multisection course with common exams and must address the same topics with his students as his colleagues address in their sections of the course. However, he finds that if his students have misconceptions, especially in fundamental areas, they are not able to follow his lectures very well anyway. He finds it better to deal with those misconceptions with clicker questions even when doing so takes class time.

Other instructors are satisfied with covering less material because they believe that teaching methods that actively engage students with course material are more effective in the long term than less engaging methods that allow for more time-efficient coverage of content. These instructors would often rather have students master fewer topics through engaged, active learning than have students be familiar with, but not fully understand, more topics. Mary Burke, who teaches biological science courses at Oregon State University, says that "sometimes less is more." She is glad to spend extra time on difficult concepts, as long as those concepts are important. Her department has had a conversation about prioritizing topics in her course, which has helped her pace her course appropriately.

Barbara Reisner, who teaches chemistry at James Madison University, finds that by including clicker questions in class sessions, she is not always able to discuss all possible examples within each topic but can cover all the topics on her syllabus. She might have six examples for a topic and discuss only three of them during class. Multiple examples within a topic allow students to begin to see patterns and more abstract structures, so there is a downside to not discussing as many examples during class. However, Reisner finds that providing students with a good foundation during class enables them to figure out any remaining examples on their own after class. Her homework assignments provide students with this opportunity.

Other instructors find that including clicker questions and small-group and classwide discussions in their courses does not prevent them from including as many topics in their courses as they would without those activities. Crouch and Mazur (2001) describe moving the transfer of information to preclass reading assignments, which allows instructors to spend class time helping students assimilate that information. Since students struggle more with the assimilation than the transfer of information, many instructors assert that it makes sense to have students engage in the assimilation step during class, when their instructor and their peers can assist them with this difficult portion of the learning process. A number of instructors who use clickers have students complete reading assignments before class for these reasons.

For example, in the multisection chemistry course in which Ivan Shibley teaches at Penn State Berks, students read their textbooks, view lecture slides from previous offerings of the course, and take online reading quizzes before class. Class time is almost entirely devoted to working through clicker questions, usually eight to twelve questions in each seventy-five-minute period. This structure has been successful in improving attendance, in spite of the availability of lecture slides, and reducing drop-withdraw-fail rates in the course. Students are sometimes uncomfortable learning in this way initially, but Shibley says that they get used to it after a few weeks. Adam Lucas also uses online preclass reading quizzes in his mathematics courses at Saint Mary's College of California. He assigns students multiple-choice reading questions to complete before class, questions he reviews using clickers at the beginning of class. He often does not lecture at all, instead using the clicker questions to help students make sense of what was unclear to them in the reading, similar to the question-driven instruction method described in Chapter Two.

While some instructors use online preclass reading quizzes to motivate students to prepare for class, others use in-class reading quizzes facilitated by clickers. Edna Ross, who teaches psychology courses at the University of Louisville, asks a number of test-style content questions each day. Students are asked to read their textbook ahead of time, so these questions function as a test of the reading. A student who gets 90 percent of the questions asked prior to an exam correct receives three extra-credit points on the exam. At least 75 percent correct earns two bonus points, and at least 50 percent correct earns one bonus point. Ross finds that this nonpunitive grading scheme motivates students to read their textbook and attend class. She also points out the importance of teaching as if students have done the reading. Otherwise the students are less motivated to prepare properly for class.

Another response some instructors give to the coverage question is that clicker questions need not displace portions of a lecture. Instead, they can replace those portions. For example, Margaret Logan, who teaches chemistry at the State University of New York at Brockport, often uses clicker questions to have her students themselves work through an example she would have worked for them were she not using clickers. Having students work through an example takes slightly more time, but she finds the trade-off reasonable. Her course is taken by chemistry majors, premed majors, and every other student whose major requires chemistry, so there are a lot of constituencies with various content needs, increasing the pressure for her to cover lots of content quickly. However, Logan says that if she does not have some kind of active learning in her course, students will not be able to pay attention for an entire lecture anyway. She uses clickers to "change up" her lectures (Middendorf & Kalish, 1996) and maintain student attention and engagement.

Some instructors spend a relatively small percentage of their class sessions on clicker activities, but given the benefits of these questions in terms of student attendance, participation, engagement, and satisfaction, they see this class time as well spent. Since clickers take up relatively little class time for these instructors, they do not prevent these instructors from including all the course content they would otherwise. Brian Augustine, for instance, who teaches chemistry at James Madison University, says that he cannot afford not to make time for active learning in his classroom. He does not think students learn much more from a fifty-minute lecture than a forty-five-minute one, so he is comfortable spending a few minutes in each class period on clicker questions. He finds the benefits, including the ability to break up a long lecture and receive daily feedback about his students' learning, outweigh the costs, which typically consist of having students read on their own about a few topics he does not have time to cover in class.

Finally, some instructors find that they can move more quickly during class because of the feedback and data-gathering capabilities of their classroom response systems. If the results of a clicker question indicate that students understand a particular topic, the instructor can move on to the next one, saving class time. Bill Hill, who teaches psychology at Kennesaw State University, notes that a classroom response system can save time when gathering data from students for classroom experiments, as mentioned in Chapter Three. Instructors who may be hesitant to use classroom experiments and other active learning techniques because of the time required to collect and analyze classroom data might be willing to try such techniques with a classroom response system.

How much class time does a clicker question take? How many clicker questions should be used in a single class session?

Once a clicker question is posed, students typically begin answering it immediately. Naturally, they take longer to begin responding to a challenging or complicated question than to an easier or simpler one. Once they begin responding, however, most systems can collect responses from an entire class, no matter the size, in a few seconds. Thus, if students are able to decide on an answer quickly, the entire process of collecting responses and displaying results can take less than a minute.

The amount of class time a clicker question takes depends more on what instructors have their students do prior to submitting their answers and on what instructors do once they have seen the results of a clicker question. If the goal is to get a quick read on the pulse of the class, the clicker question need not take more than a minute or so. However, if an instructor wants to have students think about a question and respond to it individually, then engage in peer instruction and respond again, then participate in a classwide discussion of the question, the clicker question could occupy twenty minutes of class time or more. As a result, an instructor might ask anywhere between one and twenty clicker questions in a single class session, depending on the goals in asking those questions.

In contrast to some other teaching methods, teaching with a classroom response system can be somewhat unpredictable. An instructor might have planned to give students sixty seconds to respond to a particular question, only to find out after asking it that sixty seconds is insufficient. Or an instructor might find the results of a clicker question particularly surprising, such as when fewer students answer the question correctly than the instructor anticipates or when more students pick a particular answer choice than the instructor would have predicted. In these cases and in others, instructors might find themselves spending more time on a question than they planned. Often this extra time is well spent, however, since the need for it emerges out of demonstrated student learning needs.

Writing Questions

Where can instructors find clicker questions for use in their courses?

Some textbooks come with question banks that contain questions written intentionally for in-class use with classroom response systems. Others come with question banks featuring questions designed for other purposes, such as examinations, that instructors can adapt for use as clicker questions. Clicker question banks for some common courses in some disciplines are also available online. Some of these are organized by groups of instructors wanting to assist other instructors in getting started with clickers; others are collections of questions written and used by individual instructors interested in sharing them with colleagues. Online test banks are available in astronomy (Green, n.d.), chemistry (Ellis et al., 2000), earth sciences (Science Education Resource Center at Carleton College, 2008), physics (Pollock, n.d.), and mathematics (Zullo, Parker, & Cline, 2008), and many of these contain hyperlinks to other question banks in their respective disciplines.

The multiple-choice questions written for standardized tests, such as the subject-specific Advanced Placement exams taken by U.S. high school students, various graduate and professional school entrance exams, and licensure exams used in various fields, can also be a source of challenging and interesting questions. One benefit of using clicker questions that are similar to questions on these exams is that doing so can help prepare students to succeed on these important exams. However, these questions are not written for the purpose of engaging students in the classroom; they are written for summative assessment purposes, so their styles and structures may need to be adapted for use as clicker questions.

Many instructors routinely ask free-response and rhetorical questions during class sessions, and often these questions can be turned into effective clicker questions. Instructors who plan these kinds of questions ahead of time might benefit from looking through old lesson plans to find open-ended questions that could be converted into clicker questions. An instructor who tends to ask these kinds of questions spontaneously during class might have a teaching assistant or a student take notes during class on the free-response and rhetorical questions he or she asks. Recording questions in this way then provides the instructor with potential clicker questions for future classes.

Ron McClamrock, who uses clickers in his two-hundred-student introductory philosophy courses at the State University of New York at Albany, finds writing clicker questions intuitive given his experience with the courses. Often he finds himself simply adding answer choices to the rhetorical questions he would be asking anyway. He also says that writing in-class clicker questions is easier than writing exam questions. With clicker questions, if an answer choice or two is not worded in the precise way he had intended it, he can adapt during class.

What are some strategies for constructing answer choices for clicker questions?

One of the more challenging aspects of writing effective clicker questions is crafting answer choices that students are likely to select. An instructor might want one or two wrong answer choices to be chosen by a majority of students in order to create a time for telling. Another instructor might want more than one answer choice to be popular with students in order to have enough diversity in student perspectives to foster productive small-group or classwide discussions. Creating answer choices for clicker questions that students will choose requires instructors to know what their students understand, what they do not understand, and the kinds of misconceptions and perspectives they have. This is difficult since it involves understanding how novices approach the content of a discipline. Disciplinary experts can find it challenging to put themselves in the shoes of a novice and imagine ways in which a novice might approach a particular question or problem (Bransford, Brown, & Cocking, 2000). Thus, instructors are likely to find useful one or more of the following techniques for understanding student perspectives.

One useful way to understand the perspectives students bring to a question is to examine student responses to free-response questions asked in other contexts. For example, instructors might look at the answers, especially the wrong ones, that students provided on an exam question in a previous semester. This can shed light on the misconceptions or difficulties students have with a question or topic. Turning a few of the more popular responses to an exam question into answer choices for a clicker question can be an effective way to generate answers that students will choose. This also allows instructors to determine if the current group of students shares the same kinds of perspectives and misconceptions that past students have had.

Bruce Atwood looks to the homework problems submitted by students in his mathematics courses at Beloit College. He finds looking for potential clicker questions makes grading homework a little more enjoyable and productive. Stacy Klein regularly uses the legacy cycle (Klein & Harris, 2007) as a structure for class sessions in her biomedical engineering courses at Vanderbilt University. One component of the cycle involves students' brainstorming solutions to complex problems. She says that she learns about student misconceptions during these brainstorming sessions, and what she learns later influences her clicker questions.

A similar option is to pose an open-ended question to students during class, solicit their thoughts on the question, then use their comments to construct answer choices to a clicker question to be used later in the same course or in future courses. Since it can be difficult to take notes on student comments during a discussion while also facilitating that discussion, instructors pursuing this option might find it useful to recruit a teaching assistant or a student in the course to take notes on the discussion for later use in drafting answer choices.

Another way to learn about student perspectives on a particular topic or question is to have students respond to free-response questions before class, perhaps by e-mail or an online quiz. The instructor must then quickly identify common student responses before class and turn them into answer choices for a clicker question. This option requires students to engage with a topic before it is discussed in class by exploring it through reading or online resources, reflecting on their prior knowledge of the topic, or exploring their initial thoughts about it. It allows instructors to construct answer choices based on the perspectives expressed by the very students who will respond to the question, allowing them to more directly tailor their instruction to the learning needs of their current students.

Some instructors find it useful to have direct quotations from student responses to preclass free-response questions as answer choices. Students are sometimes more engaged in a clicker question when they know the answer choices are ones that their peers have suggested. (In most cases, instructors prefer to quote student responses, particularly incorrect responses, anonymously to avoid embarrassing students.) This approach has the additional advantage of showing students that their responses to preclass quiz questions can affect their learning experiences in class by being turned into answer choices for clicker questions. This can motivate some students to engage more seriously in these preclass quizzes.

A more immediate approach to understanding student perspectives on a question in order to construct answer choices is to pose free-response questions during class, have a few students volunteer possible answers to a question, then use the responses as answer choices for a clicker question. (See the description of Francisco Estrada-Belli's "What is a civilization?" question in Chapter Three for an example of this method.) This method relies on having a classroom response system that enables instructors to pose clicker questions on the fly during class—questions that are not entered in the system before class. Most classroom response systems provide this kind of feature. This method also requires more agile teaching than the methods already described, since instructors using it cannot predict exactly what answer choices students will generate. Instructors who like to have their class sessions planned ahead of time or are unfamiliar with a given course or group of students and thus less able to predict possible student responses might not be interested in this approach. However, instructors who enjoy class sessions that are somewhat unpredictable and want to tailor their instruction more precisely to the students in front of them during class might appreciate this method. The method also provides an option for instructors who have an interesting question they wish to pose to students as a clicker question but do not have the time or are unable to think of reasonable answer choices. Similarly, this method can be useful when instructors have no way to predict student responses to a question.

As with the method of constructing answer choices from student responses to preclass free-response quiz questions, the method of constructing answer choices from suggestions from students during class has the advantage of providing extra motivation for students to engage in a clicker question since the answer choices are drawn from their peers' suggestions. However, this method requires students to volunteer responses in front of their peers. Depending on the size of the class, this can mean they are significantly less anonymous when their responses are turned into answer choices. As a result, this method is sometimes more appropriate for use with questions for which there are no correct answers, such as opinion questions, and one-best-answer questions for which students can suggest multiple defensible answer choices.

In some disciplines, significant educational research has been conducted investigating common student misconceptions and perspectives regarding key topics in commonly taught courses, research that can inform instructors looking to construct clicker questions that uncover these common misconceptions and perspectives. For instance, the Force Concept Inventory is a multiple-choice test used in physics to assess students' conceptual understanding of topics in a typical first-year undergraduate course on forces and motion (Hestenes, Wells, & Swackhamer, 1992). Many instructors administer this test at the beginning and end of such a course as a valid and reliable assessment of student learning. One reason the test is valuable is that each question's incorrect answers are based on research on common student misconceptions of forces and motion. This inventory and the research that supports it can be useful for physics instructors who want to construct effective multiple-choice clicker questions. Similar concept inventories have been constructed in other science disciplines, and similar research on student learning has been conducted in many disciplines. Results of this research can be found in journals and other publications that focus on discipline-specific teaching and learning and in those that include work from all disciplines. McKinney (2007) provides a list of such journals.

How challenging should clicker questions be?

The difficulty of a clicker question is often shaped by the instructor's learning goals for students, as well as the function of the question in the classroom. Instructors using clicker questions to create times for telling or generate small-group or classwide discussion often find that more challenging questions engage students more in these processes. For questions used in peer instruction, for instance, the process is often more successful if one-half to two-thirds of students answer a question incorrectly on their first attempt. Many instructors interpret this as an appropriately challenging question—not so difficult that no students can answer it correctly, but difficult enough to be worth discussing in class. A clicker question asked at the end of a class session designed to assess the extent to which students understood what was discussed in class might be answered correctly by a majority of students, and that would be a sign of success for most instructors.

Keep in mind the role that simpler and easier questions can play in the classroom. A steady stream of challenging clicker questions can mentally exhaust some students. Also, if students consistently answer clicker questions incorrectly, their confidence and motivation can suffer. A few easy questions here and there can give students a break from more difficult questions and bolster their confidence by showing them what they know. Easy questions can also help warm up a group of students at the beginning of a class session for more difficult questions later in the session. For example, Steven Pollock, who teaches physics at the University of Colorado at Boulder, likes to include a few easy questions in his lessons. He says that too many tough questions can overwhelm his students, and a few easier ones boost their morale. In fact, his students do not always find his "easy" questions that easy, so these questions serve a useful purpose in letting him know what his students do and do not understand, which can sometimes be surprising.

Should instructors include answer choices such as "all of the above" and "none of the above"?

Although many multiple-choice questions require students to select a single response from a set of possibilities, other multiple-choice questions are made more difficult for students through the use of answer choices such as "all of the above," "none of the above," "two of the above," and "choices A and B are correct." Students often find questions with these answer choices more challenging because they must seriously consider each of the answer choices. In contrast, when students respond to simpler questions, they can sometimes determine the correct answer without necessarily finding reasons to eliminate all of the incorrect choices. As a result, questions that include answer choices such as "all of the above" and "none of the above" can serve a useful purpose in challenging students. These questions typically take more time to implement during class, however, since students must consider all of the answer choices.

For questions about student perspectives that have no correct answers, the "none of the above" option can often be useful. It can be difficult for instructors to predict the full range of possible student perspectives on some questions, and "none of the above" provides students with perspectives not included on the list of answer choices a way to respond honestly to the question. After seeing the results of a such a question, many instructors ask students who selected "none of the above" to share their perspectives with the class. Incorporating perspectives shared this way into subsequent versions of the same question can be a useful way to refine a question over time.

Some classroom response systems allow instructors to pose "multiple mark" questions in which students are allowed to select as many answer choices as they wish. Thus, a student responding to a question with four answer choices might choose any one of the sixteen possible combinations of these answer choices (A, B, C, D, A-B, A-C, A-D, and so on).

Mary Burke asks the question in Example 4.1 in her microbiology course at Oregon State University. Her classroom response system displays the number of students who choose each of the possible combinations of answers. For instance, four students might choose answers A and B, three students might choose answer A and C, and five students might choose answers A, B, and C. Burke uses peer instruction with this question and finds that after the first vote, students select many different combinations, but there is usually at least one choice that appears in most of the combinations chosen by students. After peer instruction time, students usually converge on the single correct combination of answers. Example 3.11 demonstrates a way to ask multiple mark questions with classroom response systems that do not allow students to select arbitrary combinations of answers. This method is more limited, since students can choose from only among the combinations the instructor specifies; nevertheless, it is often useful.

Example 4.1

During energy generation, the product(s) of cyclic photosynthesis is (are):

A. ATP.

B. oxygen.

C. NADPH.

D. hydrogen sulfide.

Mary Burke, Biological Sciences, Oregon State University

Answer choices like "two of the above" or "three of the above" require some discussion after the clicker results are collected. Some students responding "two of the above" might think that answer choices A and B are correct, whereas others might think that B and D are correct. Thus, knowing that some percentage of students chose "two of the above" does not tell instructors how well students understand a particular question. Instead, these answer choices work best for generating small-group and classwide discussion as students debate not only how many answer choices are correct but also which ones and why.

Beatty, Gerace, Leonard, and Dufresne (2006) describe a similar question style. They mention a physics question in which students are asked to identify the number of forces acting on a block in a particular situation. The question has no single correct answer because the number of forces acting on the block depends on which forces, such as the force of gravity exerted on the block by the Moon, are assumed to be ignored. Furthermore, the fact that a student responds with "four forces," for instance, does not mean that the student is thinking of four correct forces. The point of this style of question, then, is generating a classwide discussion in which students debate which forces are affecting the block.

Should instructors include "I don't know" as an answer choice?

Some instructors prefer to include "I don't know" as an answer choice since it allows students who would otherwise guess randomly a chance to express their confusion about a question.

Without an "I don't know" option, it is not clear from a set of clicker results how confident students are in their answers. A high percentage of students responding "I don't know" to a question usually indicates to an instructor that the question is so challenging that many students do not feel they know enough to attempt an answer. A low percentage of students responding "I don't know" usually indicates that students are reasonably confident in their answers, right or wrong. Either way, the "I don't know" option can provide useful information about students' confidence in their knowledge of a particular question or topic.

Including an "I don't know" option can also potentially encourage some students to take clicker questions less seriously. One can imagine a student who responds "I don't know" to just about every question instead of trying to seriously answer those questions. There is also some merit to the idea of encouraging students to keep thinking about a question until they have some idea for an answer. The "I don't know" option gives these students an excuse not to persist in the sometimes difficult task of following a line of thought to its conclusion. Furthermore, one of the reasons many instructors like to use clickers is that they encourage each student to commit to an answer. Giving an "I don't know" option allows students to respond to a question without actually committing to an answer, which limits the value of this property of classroom response systems. Some instructors prefer not to use "I don't know" options for these reasons.

For other approaches to assessing student confidence in their answers to content questions, see the discussion of confidence-level questions in Chapter Three.

Must instructors prepare clicker questions before class? Can they ask on-the-fly questions during class?

The idea of constructing answer choices to a question on the fly during class by using student suggestions is an example of a more general approach to question asking in which instructors do not plan questions. Some instructors who use clickers like the ability to ask an on-the-fly question that occurs to them during class, perhaps in response to a student comment or question.

Most classroom response systems have some capability to ask spontaneous questions during class. Some allow instructors to input questions and answer choices that are quickly turned into clicker questions. Other systems allow students to respond to generic "select A, B, C, or D" questions that instructors flesh out verbally with question stems and answer choices during class. Either way, the ability to pose clicker questions generated during class as a result of discussion can be a useful tool in support of agile teaching. A student comment might indicate an unexpected misconception to an instructor, one that can be explored through an on-the-fly question. And sometimes an instructor asks a clicker question that receives unexpected results, leading to an on-the-fly question designed to explore the reasons students chose certain answers in the first question.

Brian Augustine likes to use on-the-fly questions in his chemistry courses at James Madison University. He often asks a rhetorical question, refines it by quickly adding a few answer choices that reflect common student misconceptions, then has all of his students respond with their clickers. He considers this classroom response system feature very important. Stuart, Brown, and Draper (2004) describe the regular use of on-the-fly questions in a 140-student course on philosophical logic. One method they describe involves having a student volunteer an answer to an open-ended question, then having the other students agree or disagree with the first student's answer using their clickers. This method puts the first student on the spot to some extent, but under the right circumstances, it can be used to quickly and easily create questions.

How can instructors improve their clicker questions?

One way to improve these questions over time is to consider dropping or revising unpopular answer choices—those that are not chosen by many students. Most classroom response systems allow instructors to view the results of clicker questions after class, and unpopular answer choices can be easily identified. An answer choice not selected by many students is likely one that does not reflect student thinking well. Sometimes such an answer choice can be tweaked to bring it more in line with student thinking so that the next time the question is asked, more students select that choice, providing a better picture of student thinking. At other times, an unpopular answer choice is so inconsistent with student thinking on the question that it might as well be removed and replaced with a more useful answer choice.

Another way to improve questions is to take notes on students' comments in response to a clicker question. Constructing answer choices involves trying to predict how students might respond. It is often evident during class discussions when those predictions are off the mark. Fortunately, those discussions also usually provide insight into student thinking that can be used to improve those predictions. Sometimes student perspectives not captured by the answer choices to a clicker question emerge during discussions of the question. Other times, the reasons students provide for their answer choices can help instructors better understand student perspectives and help them refine the answer choices. Taking notes on class discussion of clicker questions, either during or after class, can provide information for sharpening these questions. Some instructors take notes informally, jotting down a few comments during a discussion that will help them revise their questions later. Others are more systematic in recording student discussion of clicker questions, taking time after each class session to record and reflect on the perspectives shared during class. Instructors might also ask a teaching assistant or a student in the class to take notes on discussions of clicker questions, notes that can be used after class to revise clicker questions.

Yet another way to improve clicker questions is to share and discuss them with colleagues interested in teaching with clickers. Some instructors like to share and receive feedback on potential questions with their colleagues before using those questions. Often colleagues can provide perspectives useful for improving the clarity of questions and the relevance of answer choices. Other instructors like to debrief with colleagues clicker questions they have used recently in the classroom. Seeking out peers' perspectives on, for instance, the class discussion that followed a particular question can be a useful way of making sense of that discussion for the purposes of improving questions.

Sharing and discussing clicker questions with colleagues in one's own discipline can be productive since those colleagues are likely to understand the content of the course in which the question is asked and to have a sense of the kinds of thinking and perspectives students are likely to bring to the question. They are often able to offer revisions to a question based on their experience teaching in the discipline. When Ivan Shibley and his colleagues at Penn State Berks decided to incorporate clicker questions in their multisection introductory chemistry course, they spent a summer writing questions collaboratively. During the semester, they frequently asked the same questions on the same day in class and discussed questions together later. They also sought feedback from a group of instructional designers who were helping them redesign their course. This process helped them refine their questions over time.

Sharing and discussing clicker questions with colleagues in other disciplines can be effective as well. These colleagues do not bring the same kind of disciplinary knowledge to these discussions, but they are often better able to imagine how students, as novices in a discipline, might approach a question. This ability to take on the perspective of a student, combined with their experience teaching (with or without clickers) in their own discipline, can help these colleagues function as educated novices, providing useful feedback on a question and its implementation in the classroom.

At the University of Minnesota at Duluth, a group of instructors from several disciplines met to share and discuss their experiences teaching with clickers. Charlene Harkins, who teaches large-enrollment nutrition courses, was one of these instructors and found it helpful to share her questions with colleagues from other disciplines. In explaining her questions to someone in another discipline, she had to be very clear with them and with herself what her goals were for her questions. She found it helpful when Shelley Smith, an instructional consultant at the University of Minnesota at Duluth, shared with the group Bloom's taxonomy of educational objectives (Anderson & Krathwohl, 2001), mentioned in Chapter Three. The taxonomy helped Harkins and others in the group determine ways to ask more challenging and effective clicker questions of their students.

At the University of Oklahoma, a group of four instructors from three disciplines who all teach statistics are leading a project funded by the National Science Foundation to develop and assess clicker questions for use in statistics courses. Teri J. Murphy and Curtis Knight are mathematicians, Michael Richman is a meteorologist, and Robert Terry is a psychologist. They write their questions collaboratively and meet weekly to discuss new questions and debrief the ones they used in class that week. Each brings a different disciplinary perspective to these discussions, and Murphy and Richman report that they have learned a lot about teaching statistics from these discussions. For instance, Richman says that Terry likes to ask questions for which there are no correct answers. Dealing with uncertainty and being clear about assumptions are important skills in statistics, and these questions help students learn these skills. Seeing Terry's clicker questions has broadened Richman's approach to the course. Many of the group's discussions center on writing effective answer choices, which Richman often finds to be the hardest part of the process. For instance, one of them might suggest a question and answer choices. The others then try to reverse-engineer the answer choices, trying to determine why students would choose each of them. They also annotate their questions and their experiences in class implementing the questions, which also helps the collaborative writing process.

STUDENT RESPONSE, PARTICIPATION, AND GRADING

The discussion here describes some common student responses to the use of classroom response systems, as well as some options for how instructors might respond to these reactions, drawn from my own experience and interviews with instructors who use clickers. Many of the points made are confirmed in research that has looked at student perceptions of classroom response systems, including Barnett (2006); Graham, Tripp, Seawright, and Joeckel (2007); Kaleta and Joosten (2007); MacGeorge et al. (2007); Nagy-Shadman and Desrochers (2008); and Trees and Jackson (2007).

How do students respond to using classroom response systems? What do they typically appreciate about clickers? What do they not appreciate?

Many students appreciate the interactive element that a response system adds to a class. They find it enlivens a class session and makes it more fun. Some of this is a function of the technology itself; many students like interactive gadgets. Some is a function of how instructors use clickers to engage their students. Students usually appreciate the feedback that a classroom response system provides on their learning, which lets them know daily what they understand in a course, what they do not understand, and where they stand among their peers. (It is also the case that students who are reminded on a daily basis just how much they do not understand in a course can become discouraged. Instructors often need to monitor these students and intervene as appropriate.) Clickers also often indicate to students that their instructors are interested in their learning and in tailoring instruction to their learning. This can help create a positive rapport between instructors and students. Students appreciate that clickers allow them to respond anonymously to questions their instructors ask since this makes it safer for them to share opinions and otherwise participate in class. Often students are hesitant to share their perspectives in class out of worry about their classmates' reactions, particularly if they are unsure of their answers to a question. Clickers allow students to participate without worrying about such matters, and students often cite this as a reason they like clickers.

If clickers are not used in ways that students perceive as beneficial to their learning, some may grumble. For instance, an instructor who uses clickers to facilitate in-class quizzes might find that students perceive the clickers as a tool for making the instructor's job easier by automating the grading of these quizzes. Since this greater efficiency does not have a direct impact on their learning in the course, students who believe that this is the only or primary reason an instructor uses clickers are likely to object to this use. Similarly, students who believe that an instructor is using clickers primarily or exclusively to enforce student attendance are likely to resent being tracked or monitored. Student objections along the lines described here are magnified if students are required to purchase clickers. They might argue, "Why should we have to spend money to help our instructor save a little time grading or enforce an attendance policy?" Instructors can certainly use clickers to make grading quizzes more efficient or to enforce attendance, but if these uses are not supplemented with other uses that more clearly benefit student learning (such as the uses outlined in Chapters One and Two), instructors are likely to encounter some student resistance.

In the case of using clickers to collect and grade student responses to in-class quizzes, one way to do so that more clearly benefits student learning is to review such quizzes immediately after administering them, using the results provided by a classroom response system to guide the review, as described in Chapter Two. Clickers enable instructors to review quizzes while the questions are fresh in the minds of students and to do so in a way that is responsive to student learning difficulties by focusing on the areas of difficulty revealed by the clicker results. Students who see instructors using clickers with quizzes in this way are often less likely to object to their use since the benefits to their own learning are clearer.

Instructors might also help students see the connection between in-class clicker questions and questions that appear on exams. Students can find it frustrating when in-class learning activities do not help them prepare for graded assessments. When they see that responding to clicker questions in class helps them prepare for higher-stakes exams, they are often more appreciative of the use of clickers. For example, Adam List includes multiple-choice conceptual questions on his chemistry exams at Vanderbilt University. Before he started using clickers, students would come to his office after an exam saying that they answered all of the procedural questions on the exam correctly but missed the conceptual ones. He finds that in-class clicker questions give his students a chance to practice these kinds of questions before exams, which they appreciate.

If students are asked to purchase their own clickers, they often expect to use them regularly during class. If clickers are used only occasionally, then these students are likely to complain about the cost. How frequently should clickers be used to avoid this issue? Anecdotal evidence indicates that using clickers a few times in a class session at least once a week during a standard semester is sufficient. This threshold likely depends on how the clickers are used. Using clickers in ways that are meaningful to students just a couple of times a week might be sufficient. Clickers used in less meaningful ways might need to be used more frequently to appear worth the cost to students.

Instructors who use clickers to engage students during class in the ways described in Chapter One sometimes encounter resistance from students whose expectations of the nature of the classroom learning experience do not align well with the active engagement that clickers can facilitate. For instance, some students believe that their instructor's role is to clearly explain course content during their lectures (Perry, 1999; Belenky, Clinchy, Goldberger, & Tarule, 1986). The student's role then is to take careful notes during class, memorize the information contained in these notes, and echo that information back to the instructor on exams. Asking such students to engage in clicker-facilitated peer instruction, for instance, clashes with their expectations for learning. Why should students discuss a question with their peers when the instructor has all the answers? Of course, peer instruction and similar small-group discussions can be effective in helping students assimilate and make sense of information for all the reasons mentioned in Chapter One. However, a student whose view of learning does not place value on these kinds of interactions is likely to resist the use of clickers, at least until he or she begins to see positive results of these kinds of in-class activities.

Adam Lucas, who teaches mathematics at Saint Mary's College of California, finds that some of his students are initially resistant to his methods of instruction, which feature clicker questions and small-group and classwide discussion. He can usually convince them of the merits of these activities and finds it important to do so since he thinks that these methods promote learning that is more like what learning looks like after college.

Students with these beliefs about teaching and learning are common in higher education, and so many instructors find it useful to convey to their students the reasons they use clickers. Often students need to be reminded of these reasons throughout a course since they often forget or are not able to fully comprehend explanations of this sort offered by instructors on the first day of class. A "syllabus reminder question" as described in Chapter Three is one way to do so. An instructor might ask the clicker question in Example 4.2. This kind of question is a little biased since it requires each student to say something positive about the use of clickers. However, discussing the results of this clicker question with students can be an effective way of helping them see value in clicker-facilitated activities. If more than a few students choose answer C, for instance, an instructor might have some of those students share with the class additional thoughts on the value of peer interactions during class. Hearing classmates describe the utility of these kinds of interactions can convince other students of the value of these interactions.

Example 4.2

Which of the following reasons for using clickers in this class is most important to you?

A. Clickers allow me to check my understanding during class.

B. Clickers help my instructor focus attention on things we don't understand.

C. Discussing clicker questions with other students helps me understand course content.

D. Clicker questions make class more lively and engaging.

Students who excel in a particular course might also resist the use of clickers. Sometimes those who readily understand material in a course dislike spending class time interacting with peers, particularly peers who do not seem to understand the course material as quickly or as well as they do. These students might dislike waiting for their peers to respond to questions they perceive as easy. They might admit that a classroom response system is an effective instructional tool for other students, while maintaining that clicker questions are a waste of their own time. Sometimes these students can be convinced that their understanding of course material is enhanced when they spend time explaining clicker questions to their peers. It is often said that one really understands a subject when one has to teach it to others. However, in some contexts, these students are correct: they do not benefit from clicker questions nearly as much as their peers do. Many instructors would argue that their responsibility as teachers is to all the students in a class, not just the ones who more readily understand course material, and so the use of clickers to engage all students more effectively is justified.

This argument is not always convincing to students. If these students answer a few clicker questions incorrectly, they are more likely to begin to see value in interacting with their peers around these questions. However, students who are resistant to clicker questions for the reasons described here and consistently answer clicker questions correctly might need to be given special roles or additional activities during class that challenge them. For instance, these students might be asked to spend peer instruction time not interacting with classmates but instead drafting more challenging clicker questions than the ones being asked during class—questions that could be shared and discussed with the instructor after class. This provides the student with productive work during class time as well as more meaningful interactions with the instructor after class.

A third group of students who might resist the use of clickers is the group that resists almost any attempt to engage them during class. These are students who sit in the back of the classroom and work crossword puzzles or check their social networking Web site profiles. They show up in class and listen to the lecture or class discussion occasionally, but they are content to stay uninvolved in the lesson. Asking these students to pay attention and answer a few clicker questions every now and then during a class session is likely to prompt some grumbling. Asking them to engage in peer instruction or some more involved learning activity is likely to prompt even greater resistance. Some of this resistance might decrease when they begin to participate in clicker-facilitated activities if they find interacting with their peers enjoyable. However, some of these students can be difficult to bring into small-group or classwide discussions. This violates the implied contract they believe is in effect in the classroom: students show up and do not make any trouble for the instructor, and in return the instructor does not demand anything of the student (Merrow & Tulenko, 2005). Making clear to students that such a contract is not in effect in one's classroom and that one expects students to be actively engaged during class and interact with their peers and their instructor can be important in bringing these students on board with clicker activities.

Some instructors share data with students showing that those who participate actively in clicker questions perform better on tests and exams in the course; this can convince some resistant students. Some instructors believe that their responsibility for engaging these students goes only so far. If they have made reasonable attempts to engage students but some students refuse to be engaged in a course, then those students must take responsibility for their decision.

What problems do instructors using clickers encounter with students not bringing their clickers to class, not taking the process seriously, or cheating with clickers? How have instructors dealt with these problems?

Some instructors experience problems with students not bringing their clickers to class. Students are more likely to remember to bring their clickers if the devices are used in every class session, if they are used in ways that seem integral to the learning experience, if they are used in their other courses, or if some portion of their grade depends on their use of clickers. Thomas Benzing, who teaches a course on environmental issues in science and technology at James Madison University, did not factor clicker use in his students' grades the first semester he used them, and a number of students chose not to use them. He found the clickers useful enough that the second time he taught with them, he assigned 5 percent of his students' course grades to attendance and participation as measured by their use of clickers. This resulted in most of his students engaging regularly with his clicker questions while keeping the stakes low.

Some instructors tell their students that if they forget their clickers or if their clickers are not working for some reason, such as a dead battery, then they can submit their answers to clicker questions on paper at the end of a class session. This provides well-meaning students who forget their clickers an option for receiving credit for their participation. Of course, this approach also creates more work for the instructor, since these students' clicker grades must be entered in a gradebook by hand. It also makes it easier for students to work a little less hard to remember to bring their clickers since they know there is an option to receive participation credit without their clickers. Furthermore, the more students who take this option in a single class session, the less informative the data collected by a classroom response system are. As a result, some instructors have strict policies about forgotten clickers, providing students with no option for receiving participation credit if they forget their clickers. Ron McClamrock instituted such a policy in his two-hundred-student philosophy course at the State University of New York at Albany. He did not enforce the policy very strictly the first semester he used it and ended up with many students who needed special treatment because they did not bring their clickers. Being clearer about this policy helped significantly during his second semester using clickers. Taking a stance like this one requires explaining the policy clearly to students at the start of a course and enforcing it strictly. Once an instructor makes a couple of exceptions, the policy becomes much more difficult to enforce.

Another way to deal with the issue of forgotten or malfunctioning clickers is to allow students to drop some of their clicker grades. For instance, if a course meets for thirty-six class sessions during a semester and each class session has an associated clicker grade, instructors might ignore the lowest four clicker grades and average the remaining thirty-two to compute students' participation grades in the course. Under this plan, if a student reports to an instructor before class that he forgot his clicker, the instructor can remind the student that the lowest four clicker scores are dropped to allow for just such an event.

Very few instructors seem to have problems with students not taking clicker questions seriously. Sometimes one or two students in a class choose nonsensical answers just to be silly, but this seems relatively rare. The prevalence of this behavior depends in part on how clickers are used in a class. If students believe that their instructors are truly interested in assessing their learning or hearing their perspectives on a topic, they are more likely to answer honestly and seriously. It can thus be important for instructors to respond in some way to the results of a clicker question, either by talking about several of the more popular or interesting answer choices or by initiating a classwide discussion about the results. This conveys to students that their opinions and perspectives are heard and relevant. The fact that students' responses to clicker questions are anonymous can minimize smart-aleck responses, since students wanting to draw attention to themselves with their nonsense responses are not able to do so directly. They must respond in some silly manner, then claim that response in front of the class when the clicker results are displayed. The fact that classroom response systems can be used to inform instructors of the answers given by particular students—that student responses need not be anonymous to instructors—also helps prevent these kinds of answers, since instructors can determine after class which students respond in such ways. Of course, if students are graded on the accuracy of their responses to questions that have correct and incorrect answers, then there is much less motivation for students to answer questions in silly or dishonest ways. (As mentioned in the discussion of student perspective questions in Chapter Three, some students who take clicker questions seriously may still be hesitant to answer opinion or personal experience questions about sensitive topics honestly knowing that their instructors can see their answers after class. This is a different issue from dishonest answers to clicker questions provided by smart-aleck students.)

The issue of cheating arises when grades are assigned in some way based on students' responses to clicker questions. Typically cheating takes the form of student A giving his clicker to student B before class, student A skipping class, and student B responding to clicker questions with both his own clicker and student A's clicker, making it appear that student A is present in class. The higher the stakes, the more likely this kind of cheating will occur. If grades based on student responses to clicker questions constitute only, say, 5 percent of a student's overall course grades, then there might not be much motivation for students to cheat in this way since absence from a single class session does not significantly alter anyone's overall course grade. If clicker grades constitute a higher percentage of students' overall course grades, say 20 percent, there might be more motivation to cheat. Incidence of cheating is also likely related to class size. In a class with fifteen students, instructors are quite likely to notice a student using two clickers. In a class with two hundred students, this behavior is more difficult to detect, although some instructors assert that they can spot it in large classes.

Most instructors tend to be clear with students at the start of a course that this kind of behavior is unacceptable, outlining appropriate punishments for students caught cheating in this way.

Edna Ross, who teaches psychology at the University of Louisville, tends not to worry about students cheating by bringing other students' clickers to class. In her smaller recitation sections, where clickers are used for quizzes, teaching assistants can monitor things well enough. During lecture, the clicker questions are such low stakes that she feels it is not worth it for the students to cheat. Ross finds it helpful to spell out the consequence for cheating on clickers very clearly on her syllabus: an F in the course is the standard penalty. Thus, for her students, the few extra-credit points are not enough to risk cheating.

Being clear about anticheating policies and enforcing them when necessary seems to prevent much of this kind of behavior. In courses where clicker grades count for relatively little of a student's overall course grade, instructors are often content to concede that some cheating will happen without being detected, knowing that it has a minor impact on student grades. However, an issue for some instructors is that requiring attendance and tracking student attendance with a classroom response system can result in problems with students who would not otherwise attend class. Charlene Harkins teaches a very large nutrition course at the University of Minnesota at Duluth. She enforces attendance by counting clicker questions toward a participation grade. She once caught two dozen of her 360 students cheating by using other students' clickers to make them appear they were present or by voting on the first clicker question of the day and then leaving.

A perhaps more serious form of cheating occurs when students share answers during in-class, clicker-facilitated quizzes and exams meant to be completed independently. Of course, this kind of behavior can occur whether or not students use clickers to respond to quiz or exam questions, and many instructors have found ways to deal with it. Clickers can actually make this kind of cheating more difficult for students since the window of opportunity to see how other students respond to quiz questions is much smaller when clickers are used. Cheating students must observe other students' answers as they are submitting them by clicker; they do not have the option of looking at another student's paper quiz to see answers to questions already answered.

Should clicker questions be included as part of students' grades?

Clicker questions used as part of a quiz or exam are certainly graded. There are also occasions when instructors provide students the opportunity to answer questions completely anonymously. In these cases, grading clicker questions is impossible. But what of questions used primarily to engage students or provide formative assessment on student learning that do not require complete anonymity?

Assigning a grade to student responses to clicker questions tends to encourage students to bring their clickers to class and participate by answering questions. Many, but certainly not all, instructors find it necessary to assign grades to clicker questions in order to generate the participation levels they want. One of those who does not is Philippa Levine, who teaches a 180-student history course at the University of Southern California. Even without grading her clicker questions in any way, which allows her to ask students sensitive questions they might not answer without the condition of anonymity, 99 percent of her students participate. Robert Bartsch teaches psychology at the University of Houston at Clear Lake. His students do not purchase their own clickers; instead, he brings a set of them to class for their use every day. As a result, his clicker questions are completely anonymous. About 80 percent of his students respond to clicker questions in any given class session. Given his use of clickers and his goals for the course, he is satisfied with that participation rate.

Some instructors prefer to grade clicker questions on effort by assigning full credit for any answer submitted by students, regardless of the answer's accuracy. This rewards students for participating in clicker questions. Other instructors prefer to grade clicker questions on accuracy by assigning full credit to correct answers submitted by students and no credit to incorrect answers. This policy provides a strong incentive for students not only to participate but to answer questions correctly. Other instructors prefer a mixed approach, assigning full credit to correct answers and partial credit to incorrect answers. This rewards students for participating and provides incentive for students to answer questions correctly. (The section on grading schemes later in this chapter discusses these and other schemes.)

One rationale for motivating students to participate in clicker questions by assigning grades to those questions is that instructors see participation in questions and associated in-class activities as beneficial to student learning. Although grades are usually used primarily to evaluate student learning, they are also often used to promote behaviors seen as beneficial to this learning. Thus, student homework is graded not only to evaluate student performance on homework questions but also to motivate students to complete assignments that will help them make sense of course material. Without assigning a grade for homework assignments, many students would not complete the assignments and thus miss out on valuable learning experiences.

In the same way, many instructors assign a grade to clicker questions to motivate students to engage in an activity that helps them make sense of course material. Kristen Hessler, who teaches philosophy at the State University of New York at Albany, finds that although her students are motivated to get good grades in her courses, they do not always make the connection between attending class regularly and doing well in the course, so she assigns a grade to clicker questions. This helps students see a more direct connection between attending class and doing well in the course. Also, by having multiple clicker questions spread throughout a class session, students are not able to just take a quiz and leave; they must stay for the entire class session. One of the reasons clickers work well for motivating student attendance, participation, and engagement is that they hold students accountable for their behaviors. Each student's clicker responses can be tracked by an instructor, providing a greater degree of accountability on a day-to-day basis.

Other instructors feel that they have the responsibility to provide opportunities for learning and students have the responsibility to take the initiative and participate in those opportunities. Students are welcome to participate in classroom learning experiences, but a student who decides not to participate in clicker questions and associated activities that might benefit his or her learning is the one missing out and is the one responsible for suffering any consequences of that decision. As a result, these instructors do not see the need to motivate student participation in clicker questions by assigning grades or points to the questions.

They feel that students should motivate themselves to participate in productive ways.

Another primary rationale for motivating students to participate in clicker questions by assigning a grade to these questions is that instructors who make decisions about the flow of a class session based on the results of clicker questions—that is, instructors who practice clicker-based agile teaching as described in Chapter Two—often want to make sure that the data they collect about student learning or student perspectives from clicker questions are reliable. Suppose that the results of a clicker question indicate that 60 percent of students have a particular misconception about a topic. This would argue for spending more time on that topic during class. However, if only half the students in a class responded to the question, then all an instructor really knows is that 30 percent of students have that misconception. The instructor does not know if the half of the class who did not respond shares that misconception. In this case, it is less clear that more class time should be spent on this topic. As a result of cases like this one, instructors often want to hear from as many of their students in response to a clicker question as possible so that they can make more informed classroom decisions. Assigning grades or points to questions motivates students to answer those questions, and so these instructors include clicker questions in students' course grades to increase the utility of the data they gather from clickers.

On the other hand, some instructors feel that if students choose not to participate in clicker questions, then they are in effect opting out from having a voice in the classroom. As a result, these instructors feel that they do not have as much responsibility to craft a class session that is responsive to these students' learning and perspectives. They make their agile teaching decisions based on the responses from students who choose to provide such responses. Students who opt out of this process might or might not benefit from the classroom decisions these instructors make, of course. If by opting out, they do not learn as much during class, then they must take responsibility for that decision.

Yet another reason to use grades to motivate students to participate in clicker questions is that students who have taken the time to think about and commit to an answer to a clicker question individually and independently are more prepared to engage in subsequent small-group or classwide discussions. They have had the chance to organize their thoughts on the question, so they are likely to have more to bring to such discussions. They have already committed to answer by pressing a button on their clickers, so they are more likely to want to defend their answer through argument and reason during subsequent discussions. As a result, the quality of these discussions, and thus the learning experience for all students in the class, depends in part on the number of students who respond to prediscussion clicker questions.

Many instructors view themselves as responsible for creating learning environments in class that benefit as many students as possible, and so assigning grades to clicker questions makes sense as a way to augment the learning experience for all students. This rationale is similar to one often used to justify participation grades in discussion-oriented courses. The more students who actively participate in discussions, the better the learning experience is for all students. In the same way, motivating students to respond to clicker questions benefits not only the learning of the students who respond but the learning of their peers.

A counterpoint to this line of thought is that a student's grade in a course should reflect that student's performance: his or her participation, learning, and mastery of course material. Using grades to motivate behaviors in one student (answering clicker questions prior to class discussions) that benefit other students can be seen as diluting the evaluative aspect of course grades. For example, suppose a very bright student clearly shows on quizzes and exams that she has mastered the course material yet she does not participate in clicker questions during class. Her lack of participation might detract from the learning opportunities for other students, but should she be penalized for not participating when it is clear from her test scores that she understands the course material? An instructor's views on the meaning of student grades plays an important role in the decision to assign grades to clicker questions.

Other reasons instructors often provide for not grading clicker questions are more logistical in nature. Although most classroom response systems automate much of the grading process, grading clicker questions usually takes some amount of administrative work. Most classroom response systems have tools for designating answer choices to clicker questions as correct or incorrect, either before or after the questions are asked during a class session. Once these systems "know" which answers are correct, they can usually generate reports after class showing each student's score on the clicker questions used during that session. Although some systems have sophisticated internal gradebooks that instructors can use to track student performance, often instructors prefer to take the scoring data generated by these systems and export this information to a gradebook in a spreadsheet program or in an online course management system. Different systems have different tools for exporting data that require different amounts of work on the instructor's part. Usually these systems allow batch processing of grades, meaning that the amount of work required in exporting or otherwise dealing with scoring data does not increase with the number of students in a course. Batch features keep these processes from being too cumbersome, but managing the scoring data generated by classroom response systems usually takes some instructor time. Some instructors view this as too burdensome and thus do not grade student responses to clicker questions.

Another administrative challenge to grading clicker questions is dealing with students who forget to bring their clickers to class or bring clickers that fail to work for some reason. One option for handling students like this is to have them submit their responses on paper, but that means these students' scores must be processed by hand. If this occurs with one or two students over the course of a semester, that does not add much to the administrative task of managing clicker scores. However, handling these exceptions does not scale well, so that many students requiring this kind of processing can add significantly to the time needed to track clicker scores. It can be helpful to have clear policies about forgotten or malfunctioning clickers that are communicated to students early in a course and enforced fairly rigorously to prevent these issues from becoming problematic for an instructor.

Similarly, grading clicker questions can involve responding to students who dispute their clicker scores. Assuming that an instructor can communicate students' clicker scores to them, perhaps through the gradebook tool of an online course management system, some students might find reason to argue with particular clicker scores. In some cases, they will argue that they actually answered particular questions recorded as unanswered by the classroom response system. These disputes can be difficult to resolve because there is usually no paper trail that can be used to verify such a claim. In other cases, students will disagree with the instructor about the correct answers to particular questions. Since instructor and student can discuss reasons for and against the disputed answer choices, these disputes can be easier to resolve and can in fact turn into learning opportunities for both student and instructor. But if an instructor has already recorded clicker scores for a group of students based on the assumption that, say, answer B was correct and then becomes convinced by a student that answer choice C is also correct, the process for revising the scores of the other students who chose C can be time-consuming.

It should also be noted that classroom response systems, like any other technology, fail to work from time to time. Some systems are more reliable than others, and instructors with experience using particular systems are often able to prevent or fix technical problems. However, since these systems can fail, student responses and scoring data can sometimes be lost. Instructors wary of dealing with bugs and technical problems sometimes choose not to grade student responses to clicker questions for this reason. It is one thing to ask a couple of students whose clickers are malfunctioning to submit their responses on paper; it is quite another to ask an entire class of students to do so because of malfunctioning software.

What are some effective grading schemes for clicker questions?

Some instructors prefer to grade clicker questions on effort, assigning equal credit to all answer choices, right or wrong. Others grade students on the accuracy of their answers, assigning full credit to correct answers and no credit for incorrect ones. Many instructors feel it is inappropriate to grade students on the correctness of their responses to clicker questions during the same class sessions in which the topics of those questions are introduced to the students. These instructors prefer to grade questions on effort in order to motivate students to engage with new topics and for formative assessment purposes; they then grade later assignments on accuracy once students have had opportunities to master those topics.

Another argument against grading clicker questions on accuracy is that it can give students who correctly answer critical thinking questions the false sense that they have mastered those questions, when in fact it is often quite possible to answer such questions correctly without fully understanding all the reasons for and against the answer choices. Grading these questions on accuracy can lead some students to miss the fact that it is the small-group or classwide discussions of the questions where real learning takes place since it is during those discussions that students get the chance to sharpen their critical thinking skills. Thus, some would argue, as Beatty, Leonard, Gerace, and Dufresne (2006) do, that grading clicker questions, especially critical thinking questions, on accuracy can lead students to fail to realize the important role that critical reasoning plays in the learning process and in the disciplines.

Grading clicker questions on accuracy increases the pressure students feel to master course material. Some instructors want their students to feel this pressure, since it can motivate them to seriously engage with course material as it is being presented during class. Others dislike creating high-pressure classroom environments and prefer to grade clicker questions on effort, not accuracy. Of course, if students would reasonably be expected to have mastered particular course content by the time clicker questions on that content are asked, then it may be more appropriate to grade on the accuracy of answers. For instance, some instructors begin class with a reading quiz administered by clickers. The questions on these quizzes are often fairly straightforward ones that students who do the reading can easily answer. An instructor might reasonably grade these questions on accuracy to provide additional motivation for students to complete their reading assignments. As another example, some instructors like to ask a couple of questions that are graded on accuracy at the end of a class session as a way to motivate students to make sense of course content during that session. These instructors often feel that students should understand such course content by the end of a class session, so grading end-of-class questions on accuracy is appropriate.

Mary Burke teaches a 180-student microbiology course at Oregon State University. She grades her in-class clicker questions on accuracy. She does not want students to click just any answer, and grading clicker questions provides them the motivation to take the questions seriously. Since she asks questions on topics that have just been covered in lecture and since the students can consult their notes, she usually aims for at least three-quarters of her students to answer the questions correctly. When she achieves this success rate, she still reviews the correct answers so students have the chance to hear her explanation of the question. If fewer than half of the students answer correctly, she usually has them discuss the question in pairs and asks the question again. This usually increases the students' success rate and in the process offers students a second chance to get credit for that question.

Linda Johnston, who teaches nursing at the University of South Carolina at Aiken, grades her clicker questions on accuracy as well. She typically asks four graded questions during each class period: two at the start that quiz students on the reading assignment for the day and two at the end to assess students' understanding of the lecture. Students score one point each for correct answers and no points for incorrect answers. Altogether these questions count for 5 percent of her students' course grades.

A variation on grading on accuracy is the scheme Dennis Jacobs of Notre Dame University uses, the one described in the discussion of confidence-level questions in Chapter Three. Under this scheme, students are asked not only to answer content questions but to report their confidence in their answers. Students who are highly confident and correct score the most points, students who are highly confident and incorrect score the least points, and students who lack confidence in their answers score somewhere in the middle, regardless of the accuracy of their answers. (See Chapter Three for a discussion of this scheme.)

Another option is to use a mixed approach, assigning full credit to correct answers and partial credit to incorrect ones. This scheme strikes a balance between grading on effort and grading on accuracy, rewarding students who master course material but also rewarding, though to a lesser extent, students who participate in clicker questions. Some instructors implement a twist on this scheme by assigning full credit to incorrect answers and extra credit to correct answers. This rewards students for participating, does not penalize them for answering incorrectly, and motivates them to answer questions correctly as often as possible. Instructors who are comfortable awarding extra credit might find this scheme strikes the right motivational balance.

Instructors often use different grading schemes that work best in their individual classrooms. For example, Anthony Crider uses a mixed grading scheme in his astronomy courses at Elon University. He assigns 10 percent of his students' course grades to clicker questions. Each class period counts the same in this 10 percent, no matter how many clicker questions are asked in a class. Students get half credit for answering incorrectly and full credit for answering correctly. The questions are drawn from their readings, including lecture notes made available before class, and Crider makes most of his clicker questions available to students before class. Once he explains this to his students, they seem to understand that it is their responsibility to prepare for class and do well on these questions.

Other instructors have similar grading schemes. Barbara Reisner gives 90 percent partial credit for incorrect answers in her chemistry courses at James Madison University. Altogether, clicker questions compose 5 percent of her students' course grades, and students get to "drop" 20 percent of their clicker grades automatically to account for absences, forgotten clickers, technical difficulties, and the like. Another chemistry instructor, Margaret Logan of the State University of New York at Brockport, gives 80 percent credit for wrong answers. She uses clicker questions during thirty-six class sessions each semester, counts each day's clicker score equally no matter how many questions were asked, and drops the lowest six days' scores for each student. Her clicker questions contribute 9 percent of her students' course grades.

Kristen Hessler uses a slightly more complicated mixed grading scheme in her philosophy courses at the State University of New York at Albany. Clicker questions count for 20 percent of her students' overall course grades. Each class session's clicker questions are always worth ten points. Students earn six of those points just by answering all questions during the class session. Students failing to answer any one clicker question during a class session receive zero points out of six for this portion of their clicker grade. Four of the ten points available in each class session are reserved for answering two designated clicker questions correctly. Hessler designs these clicker questions to be of a difficulty level appropriate to where the students are in their understanding of a topic. A start-of-class reading question graded on accuracy might not be very difficult, but an end-of-class question on a topic students explore during class might be more difficult. Given the difficulty level of these questions and the fact that students can talk about the questions with each other and consult their notes and readings, usually fewer than half of her students miss these questions. Hessler's students are allowed to drop the four lowest scores in this set, allowing them to miss four class sessions without penalty. Hessler finds that this grading system motivates students to prepare for and engage in class.

Instructors choosing to grade clicker questions on effort, accuracy, or some mix of both must also decide how clicker scores contribute to the overall course grades. Many instructors choose to have clicker scores contribute only minimally to overall course grades, perhaps constituting 5 or 10 percent of the course grade. This keeps the use of questions from becoming high-pressure experiences for students and minimizes student motivation for cheating with clickers. Having clicker scores determine a higher percentage of the overall course grade, say 20 or 25 percent, provides more motivation for students to participate in clicker questions and associated activities.

Other instructors choose to have clicker scores contribute only extra credit toward an overall course grade, perhaps an extra 3 to 5 percent, so that students have some incentive to answer clicker questions but are not penalized for failing to do so. Thomas Palmeri teaches psychology at Vanderbilt University and uses the following grading scheme. A student who answers at least 75 percent of the clicker questions in a semester (right or wrong) receives 2 bonus points toward the 180 total points available in the course. About seventy out of his seventy-five students usually obtain these points. Before he implemented this system, about half of Palmeri's students did not use clickers during class.

Instructors must also decide whether to weigh each clicker question identically or to weigh the set of questions asked in each class session identically. The former option implies, for instance, that a student who misses a class session in which ten clicker questions are asked loses more points than a student who misses a class session in which two clicker questions are asked, since each question contributes equally to overall course grades. The latter option implies that these two students are penalized the same amount since each student missed a single class period. Many classroom response systems generate data on student responses to clicker questions at the end of each class session, so the latter option is usually relatively easy to implement. Some response systems make it simple to aggregate clicker responses across multiple class sessions, facilitating the former option.

Instructors who grade clicker questions on effort also have the option of penalizing students who fail to reach a certain threshold of questions answered in a semester. For example, an instructor might tell students that if they fail to answer at least 80 percent of the clicker questions asked in a course (or if they fail to answer the clicker questions asked during at least 80 percent of the class sessions in a semester), then five points will be deducted from their final course grade. This is a punitive version of the grading scheme Thomas Palmeri uses, described above.

An instructor's choice of grading scheme—one of those described here or some other scheme—depends largely on the kind of classroom environment the instructor wants to create and the motivational profile of the students involved. Some instructors strive to create low-pressure classroom environments in which students are free to take the time they need to struggle to understand course material. These instructors often grade their students' responses to clicker questions on effort, not accuracy, if they grade them at all. Some students respond well to this approach, but others do not, taking the clicker questions less seriously because all answers receive full credit. Other instructors prefer to challenge students regularly during class and see higher-stakes clicker questions as a useful tool in keeping students on their toes. These instructors often grade on accuracy, not effort. Some students rise to this kind of challenge, of course, but others find a high-pressure environment overwhelming. Instructors deciding on grading schemes must consider not only the kind of classroom environment they wish to create but also what kinds of rewards and incentives motivate their students.

CLASSROOM CHOICES

How long should students be given to submit their answers to a clicker question? When should an instructor call time and end voting?

How much time to allow students to respond to a clicker question depends, of course, on the nature of the question. Students can respond in mere seconds to some questions; other questions can require several minutes. The challenge inherent in this issue is addressing the fact that some students will respond more quickly to some questions than other students will. The variance in the length of time it takes students to respond to a clicker question can be small for some questions, particularly some recall and opinion questions that most students answer quickly and some critical thinking questions that most students take a while to answer. However, for many questions, this variance can be quite large. For example, students who possess clear understandings of the concepts assessed in questions like the ConcepTests described in Chapter Three are often able to answer these questions quickly, whereas students without those conceptual understandings might take quite a while to decide on answers to these questions.

Instructors asking clicker questions are often faced with the tough decision of determining the best time to end the voting for a question. Calling time too soon prevents some students from having the time they need to finish grappling with a tough question. If done repeatedly, it can also result in students' learning to rush to conclusions without taking the time for proper reasoning. However, if too much time is provided to respond, students who answer quickly can become bored or frustrated with their slower classmates. In addition, some students spend more time on a question than they really should, agonizing over a decision that they should be able to come to fairly quickly given their current knowledge of course material.

Some instructors wait patiently until every student has responded to a question before closing the voting. Other instructors wait until a certain percentage of students respond, perhaps 80 or 90 percent, and then announce to the class that voting will end in a few seconds. Since a few students tend to forget to submit their answers after choosing them, it is often helpful for an instructor to make some kind of announcement just before ending voting to remind these students to submit their responses. Some instructors use the timer features common in classroom response systems. These features allow instructors to designate how many seconds or minutes students have to respond to a clicker question, and they display some sort of countdown during the voting to let students know how much time remains before voting closes. Sometimes instructors decide before class how much time to allocate to each clicker question and use timers to enforce those decisions. However, many response systems allow instructors to start the countdown at any point during the voting, so instructors often have the option of waiting until a certain percentage of students have replied, then starting the timer to make sure the remaining students reply soon. Some instructors who teach classes with hundreds of students find these countdown timers invaluable in keeping students on track during class.

Not only must instructors decide how much time to allow students to respond to a clicker question, but they must also decide how to manage the students who respond quickly to a question that takes other students much longer to answer. Although some of these students use the extra time to continue thinking about the question at hand, review their notes, or look up examples in the reading, others tend to use this extra time less effectively, choosing instead to daydream or talk about off-topic matters with their neighbors. Other students can be frustrated at having to wait for their peers to respond and spend this extra time fuming at their instructor. One option for engaging fast responders is to walk over to the students and discuss the question at hand with them, asking them about the reasons they have for their answers and perhaps challenging those reasons in appropriate ways. Another option is to encourage fast responders to discuss the question and their answers with each other if they have not already done so, although instructors who want to see the results of students' individual and independent answers to a clicker question before allowing them to engage in any kind of small-group discussion would find this option less useful. A third option is to give the fast responders a task that requires them to take another look at the question at hand, perhaps asking them to write down reasons that the answers they did not choose are incorrect. Another option is to give them a question or task that prepares them for the next part of class. Of course, sometimes a little downtime during class can be useful. Students who respond to clicker questions quickly might appreciate the chance to relax for a minute or two as a way to gather their thoughts for what comes next.

One of the advantages of teaching with clickers is that clickers provide a mechanism for all students to respond to a question posed by their instructor. Moreover, classroom response systems let instructors know how many of their students have responded at any given time. When using the more traditional method of posing a question and then calling on a student volunteer to respond, instructors cannot be sure how many of the students who do not volunteer to respond have had a chance to formulate a response to the question by the time the first volunteer is called on. So as difficult as it can be to decide when to end the voting on a clicker question, instructors using clickers have some useful data with which to make that decision.

Should students be shown the results of a clicker question? Or should instructors view the results of clicker questions without showing them to students?

If more than one answer choice is chosen by a significant number of students, then showing these results to students can demonstrate that the question is a challenging one and worth discussing further. Some students will want to know why so many of their peers answered the question differently than they did, and so sharing results can encourage students to consider answer choices that they did not choose initially. Since instructors often respond to results such as these by having their students engage further with the question at hand (whether or not the question has a single correct answer or multiple reasonable answers), it can be very helpful to show students these results.

Student perspective questions often produce mixed results, and thus the results to these questions are often shared with students for the reasons outlined above. However, if one of the answer choices for a student perspective question is clearly more popular than the others, then an instructor might not want to show these results to the students. Students might find it disturbing that so many of their peers share some common experience or opinion.

Showing the students that they lack a variety of perspectives on a particular topic can sometimes inhibit students' discussion of that topic. If a student feels that all of her peers agree with her on a particular issue, why would she want to discuss it with them? Nevertheless, it can often be useful to let students know how their peers responded to a question, regardless of the outcomes, in an effort to increase mutual understanding in a class. The decision to share results from a student perspective question depends largely on the goal an instructor has in asking the question.

The ways that students interpret the results of content questions are different from the ways they interpret the results of student perspective questions. The following discussion explores the choice to share results of content questions and assumes that the clicker questions have correct answers.

If one of the answer choices is clearly more popular than the others and an instructor shows these results to the students, many of the students will likely infer that the popular answer is the correct one. Some students who believe they know the correct answer to a clicker question are less likely to listen to or engage in any discussion of the question, assuming they understand everything there is to understand about a question simply because they know the correct answer. That assumption is often not a valid one, of course. Thus, instructors who want to engage their students in further discussion of the question might not show them results such as these.

If the question has a single correct answer and the popular answer is the correct one, then, as mentioned in the discussion of agile teaching in Chapter Two, instructors might want to hear from some students to determine if they understand the question as well as the clicker results would indicate. If they do not (which might be the case if many of the students understand just enough about the question to answer correctly without understanding the question completely), then having the students spend more time discussing the question might be productive. In this case, showing the results of the clicker question might mean fewer students engage seriously in these further discussions. But if an instructor determines that the students actually understand the question as well as these results would indicate, then sharing these results with the students can be empowering. It affirms those students who answered the question correctly and warns students who answered incorrectly that most of their peers understand the topic more accurately than they do.

If the question has a single correct answer and the popular answer is incorrect, then instructors likely want to have the students spend more time discussing it. If instructors reveal the results at this point, some students will assume that the popular answer is the correct one and be less inclined to engage in any discussion. If instructors have the students discuss the question further and vote again with their clickers, they might find that even more students choose the same wrong answer out of peer pressure. To prevent that, instructors who show students these kinds of results might let the students know that most of them answered incorrectly. The students will likely find this surprising and be interested in discussing the question further. They will, of course, know that the popular answer can be eliminated as the correct one in subsequent discussions, but some instructors would be comfortable making that trade-off in order to have them take the question more seriously. Another option in this case is not to show the students the results of the initial clicker question. This means that the instructor knows that most of the students missed the question, but the students will not and, as a result, will be more inclined to continue discussing the question.

In summary, if the results of the clicker question are mixed, there are some good reasons for showing students these results. If one of the answer choices is more popular than the others, it is often not helpful to show students the results if instructors plan to have them engage with the question further. The choice of strategy depends in part on the capabilities of the classroom response system in use. If the system makes it difficult for an instructor to see the results of a clicker question while hiding those results from the students, then instructors will likely find themselves showing their students clicker results regularly. If that is the case, then for questions where one answer choice is more popular than the others, instructors might want to keep students guessing as long as possible as to whether the popular answer is correct. If the popular answer turns out to be incorrect even occasionally, students will be more inclined to engage further with this kind of question since they will be less inclined to assume that popular answers are correct ones.

If the classroom response system makes it easy for instructors to decide on the fly whether to share results with their students, then they might choose to share those results when they are mixed and hide them when one answer is more popular than the others. In this case, students will likely deduce that their instructor's decision to hide the results means that either most of them are correct or most of them are wrong. Since they will not know which of those two possibilities is in effect for any given clicker question, however, they will likely engage in follow-up discussion of the question with interest in an effort to determine to which case the question belongs.

For clicker questions with correct answers, at what point should instructors indicate which answer choice is correct?

Many classroom response systems allow instructors to designate for each clicker question an answer choice as correct. After student responses have been collected and the results tallied and displayed, these systems can signify the correct answer for the students with some visual cue, perhaps by placing a check mark next to the answer or a box around it. Instructors also have the option, naturally, of indicating correct answers verbally during class.

Some instructors choose to indicate the correct answer to a clicker question immediately after the results are displayed to the students. This can add a little dramatic flair to the display of the results: "Here's the bar chart, and, as you can see, only 25 percent of you were correct." It also gives the students rapid feedback on their learning; students are made aware as soon as possible whether their answers were right or wrong. Some students find this motivational, particularly if they find out that their answers were wrong. These students are often eager to know why their answers were wrong and why the correct answer was the right one.

When some students learn the correct answer to a clicker question, however, they disengage with any subsequent discussion of the question. Incorrectly assuming that they fully understand the question because they know which answer choice is the correct one, these students do not see the value in listening to others—their instructors or their peers—discuss the question further. They might be less likely to ask follow-up questions, and they might be less likely to continue arguing in favor of other answer choices, even when continuing such debates might help them more deeply understand the topic. Certainly not all students disengage when a correct answer to a clicker question has been indicated, but some might.

Therefore, instructors interested in using a clicker question to generate small-group or classwide discussion might prefer to delay revealing the correct answer until after those discussions have had a chance to play out. For example, if initial clicker results indicate that students are split among three answer choices, an instructor might facilitate a classwide discussion in which the students debate the merits of each of the choices. If the discussion goes well, the correct answer can become apparent to most students during the course of the discussion as the strength of the arguments in favor of that answer choice wins converts. Were the instructor to reveal the correct answer immediately after showing the results of the question, it might be more difficult to engage students in such a productive discussion.

Instructors not as interested in generating discussion of a clicker question, however, often use correct answer indicators. For example, Ivan Shibley does so in his chemistry courses at Penn State Berks. He finds that since his students find the course content so challenging, they want to know immediately whether they are correct. The correct answer indicator also saves some class time by eliminating the need to have students discuss how they arrived at the correct answer. Since Shibley often asks several questions on the same topic, students who get a question wrong and are not likely to ask questions about it (because they know they are wrong from the indicator) get the chance to continue exploring the topic in a follow-up question. Students who see the correct answer and overestimate their understanding of the topic (thinking that since they know the correct answer they fully understand the question, even when they may not) are tested on that understanding by a follow-up question.

SMALL CLASSES

What advantages and challenges are there to using clickers in small courses?

Instructors teaching small courses usually have more options for engaging and assessing students than instructors teaching large-enrollment courses do, so it is often not clear what advantages clickers offer in the small class environment. However, even in small classes, having every student participate in a single class session can be a challenge. For instance, Anthony Crider teaches relatively small astronomy courses, often with thirty students each, at Elon University. Using clickers helps him hear from all of his students, which is difficult to do otherwise. Bruce Atwood, who teaches twenty-student mathematics courses at Beloit College says is it difficult to engage twenty students at once. Clickers give him a useful tool for doing so.

Clickers not only allow all students to respond to a question; they allow those students to do so independently and, to a degree, anonymously, which can be useful when using clickers to generate discussion. Independent and anonymous responses to a question can be collected using other means—for instance, by asking students to write their responses to a question on slips of paper that are passed to the instructor, who reads them aloud to the class—but clickers provide a convenient mechanism for doing so. The need for having students formulate responses to a question before hearing their peers' responses may be less acute in smaller courses where students are often more likely to be engaged in classwide discussions in productive ways, but even in small classes, some students are likely to sit back and listen to their peers' responses before trying to construct their own. Clickers allow instructors of small courses a way to deal with this challenge.

Similarly, small courses often allow instructors to generate classroom environments that make it safer for students to share their perspectives, including those that involve minority viewpoints and potentially wrong answers, decreasing the need for providing students a way to respond to questions anonymously. However, for some questions, particularly about sensitive topics, the anonymity that clickers provide can be useful. In fact, sometimes students in smaller courses are more hesitant to share their perspectives with their classmates than students in larger courses since students in smaller courses are more likely to know each other. The anonymity that clickers provide can be particularly useful in these situations. Teresa Cosby notes the anonymity that clickers provide students to be a key reason to use them in her fifteen-student upper-level political science courses at Furman University, particularly when sensitive topics such as abortion, same-sex marriage, capital punishment, and race are discussed. The anonymity that clickers provide makes it much more likely that her students will answer these questions honestly. That in turn makes the clicker results more useful in helping students understand and potentially value each other's views.

However, in a small class, students are better able to guess which of their peers responded in particular ways to a clicker question based on the results displayed to the class. For instance, if 20 percent of a class of fifteen students responds in a certain way, that means that three of the fifteen students responded in that way. If the students in the class know each other sufficiently well, they may be able to guess who those three students are. Those guesses might be right or wrong; either way complicates the issue of anonymity.

Furthermore, there can be more pressure in smaller courses than in larger ones for students to provide answers to questions, particularly opinion questions, with which they think their instructor agrees even when those answers are not the students' honest responses. Clickers used in a fully anonymous mode, in which even the instructor does not know the individual answers provided by each student, can offer students an opportunity to answer questions completely honestly, an opportunity that can be difficult to replicate without clickers.

Some classroom response systems provide instructors the option to see the individual answers of students during class, either as the students are submitting their responses or after the responses have been collected. In a small class in which the instructor knows the students fairly well, this information can be used to call on students during class. For example, an instructor might say to a student, "Jane, I see here that you selected answer B for this question. Would you mind sharing with the class why you selected that answer?" Although instructors in larger courses can use this tool to help them decide which students to call on during a classwide discussion, doing so without having established a productive rapport with students can lead to some students resenting being "cold-called" in class. Since establishing that rapport (and, for that matter, even learning student names) is easier in a small course, some instructors might find this technique more appropriate to smaller classes.

An exception to this idea might be law school classes, which have a tradition of instructors cold-calling students and challenging them to defend their answers to questions. One challenge of this technique, often referred to as the Socratic method, is that instructors do not usually know a priori how a given student will respond to a question. According to Brian Fitzpatrick of the Vanderbilt University School of Law, by asking all students to respond to a clicker question, then using the classroom response system to identify students who selected particular answer choices, an instructor can be more selective regarding which students to call on. For instance, if an instructor would prefer to call on a student with a response that is close to the correct answer but not quite correct, using a classroom response system in this way would allow the instructor to make sure such a student is called on.

An additional advantage clickers offer to instructors teaching smaller courses is that they can be used to help make participation grades, a frequent component of small courses, more objective. Since response systems can be used to track student responses to clicker questions asked during class, the grading schemes discussed here can be used to provide relatively objective measures of student participation.

CHAPTER FIVE

TECHNICAL AND LOGISTICAL CHOICES

TECHNICAL CHALLENGES

How often do technical problems prevent classroom responses from working? How can instructors deal with technical difficulties that arise in the classroom?

As with any other instructional technology, a variety of technical problems can occur when using classroom response systems: defective clickers, defective receivers, incompatibilities between clickers and receivers, incompatibilities between a receiver and an instructor's computer, software incompatibilities, difficulties registering student clickers so that instructors can track student responses, software or hardware bugs, design features that cause problems in the classroom, and still others. Some brands of systems tend to generate more technical problems than others, and instructors new to a particular brand often experience more technical difficulties than instructors with more experience using that brand. In addition, when system vendors release new versions of their hardware and software, technical problems sometimes occur due to bugs and other issues. These are often resolved over time, but the first semester with a new system can sometimes be difficult for instructors. Technical problems with these systems seem to occur less frequently now than they did a few years ago, which is consistent with the maturation of an emerging technology.

In order to prevent as many technical problems as possible, instructors using a particular classroom response system for the first time should test the system as thoroughly as possible before using it with students. Often instructors identify problems that would be difficult to resolve during a class session but are easily resolved during testing. Tests should be conducted under conditions as close to the classroom conditions as possible, which usually means testing the system in the classroom where it will be used at least a few days in advance. Recruiting a few students to assist with these tests can be useful as well. Instructors are also advised to arrive in their classrooms early the first few days when using a new response system in order to give themselves plenty of time to set up the system and perform last-minute tests.

Although instructors can work to prevent as many technical problems as possible, not all technical problems can be predicted or prevented. Instructors may find it useful to use classroom response systems in fairly limited ways during the first few class sessions with a new system. If a technical problem prevents the system from working altogether, an instructor whose entire lesson plan is constructed around clicker questions has to do some quick thinking to compensate. If the lesson plan includes only a couple of clicker questions and the instructor has planned ways to handle those questions in case of clicker failure, technical problems need not be so traumatic. This advice can be difficult for experienced classroom response system users to follow when using a new system for the first time. Often these instructors have integrated clickers so thoroughly into their class sessions that they are hesitant to limit their use at the beginning of a semester.

When technical problems occur, many instructors experience some frustration or even embarrassment, particularly if the students seem hesitant about the use of clickers to begin with. Students are more likely to weather technical difficulties well if their instructors remain calm and in control of the situation. Many instructors spend only a short time trying to troubleshoot a technical problem during class in an effort not to waste limited class time. Having a backup plan in mind and moving quickly and confidently to that plan can help instructors move past their frustration and embarrassment and help students maintain confidence in their instructors.

Instructors have a few options when technical difficulties prevent a response system from working. Depending on the nature and use of the question to be asked, some of the lower-tech options described later in this chapter can be useful. For instance, having students hold fingers in front of their chests (one finger for choice A, two fingers for choice B, and so on) can work well in a pinch since this system provides students with the opportunity to respond to a question somewhat anonymously and independently of their peers and gives an instructor a rough idea of the distribution of responses to a question (Slater, 2005). Having students submit their answers to a question in writing is another option. Analyzing responses submitted in writing takes longer, of course, and might take too much time to be conducted during a class session. However, written responses can provide instructors with information about student learning and perspectives that can be leveraged in subsequent class sessions.

A clicker question intended for use in peer instruction can still help generate discussion even if responses cannot be collected. Having students reflect individually on such a question, then discuss it in pairs, then share their thoughts during a classwide discussion can be a productive way to help them engage with course material.

If only a few students have malfunctioning clickers, instructors with a few spare clickers or replacement batteries on hand can often help those students quickly. Charlene Harkins, who teaches large-enrollment nutrition courses at the University of Minnesota at Duluth, finds that having a student come up after class to ask a question about a malfunctioning clicker gives her a chance to connect with that student—a connection that might not otherwise occur in her large classes.

If clicker questions are to be graded, then students are likely to be concerned about how a technical failure affects their grades. Reassuring students that their grades will not suffer because of a technical failure can be important in these instances. One of the advantages of not grading clicker questions is that technical failures are not as stressful to students.

How much time does it typically take for an instructor to learn to use a classroom response system? How much time is required on a daily basis to prepare to use clickers in a class session?

The time it takes an instructor to learn to use a classroom response system varies, naturally, with the instructor's computer experience and the ease of use of the system in question. Some systems are very simple with few features; an instructor with general computer experience might feel comfortable with such a system after just an hour of experimentation. Other systems are more complicated, even for relatively basic uses. For these systems, an instructor might need several hours of experimentation in addition to a well-written user's manual or the help of a colleague with experience using the system. Some systems are well inte-grated with other programs, such as Microsoft PowerPoint. An instructor already familiar with PowerPoint is likely to find such a system fairly easy to learn to use. An instructor with no PowerPoint experience, however, might find such a system even more difficult to learn, given the need to gain some familiarity with PowerPoint in addition to the classroom response system software.

Instructors who experience frustration when trying to learn a new classroom response system often do so because a feature they are interested in using is not well documented in the sys-tem's user manual or help files. In this case, finding a colleague with experience using that feature can be critical to getting past such a roadblock. At other times, bugs or software or hardware incompatibilities can prevent a system from working as described in its user manual or help files. These problems can be difficult to solve; contacting the system's vendor's technical support can be necessary in these cases. Technical support representatives are often very helpful, but they are not always able to resolve issues in as timely a fashion as instructors sometimes wish.

In general, instructors interested in learning to use a classroom response system should give themselves at least a couple of weeks before they teach their first class in which they plan to use the system. It may take only a few hours to become comfortable with the system, but one or two small issues could take a few days of back-and-forth discussions with campus or vendor technical support.

The time needed to prepare to use clickers in a single class session varies with the ease of use of the system and the complex-ity of an instructor's planned use of clickers. With some systems, inserting a few questions into an existing PowerPoint presentation, for instance, takes only a minute or two per question, particularly if those questions do not have graphical elements or specialized notation. Instructors who use the floating toolbar feature of some systems, as described in the section below about vendor selection, can present their clicker questions to students in any way they wish and so can choose a presentation method that does not take much preparation time. Instructors who ask on-the-fly questions can also prepare for class rather quickly. Inserting graphical elements and specialized notation can take time with some systems. Allocating points to the correct and incorrect answers belonging to each clicker question can also take time before class. Some classroom response systems have rather complicated mechanisms for preparing questions for class, which take some time to prepare. Others allow instructors to import questions prepared in other programs, including word processing programs and test construction programs, which can help instructors prepare for class fairly quickly.

Most instructors seem to take between ten and sixty extra minutes before class to prepare clicker questions for use in a classroom response system, depending on the factors described. Adding to this time is the time needed to write useful clicker questions. For instructors not used to writing multiple-choice questions designed to engage and assess students during class, drafting useful questions can take time. (See the discussion of writing questions in Chapter Four for advice on engaging in this process productively and efficiently.) Instructors teaching a course for which they already have clicker questions written and prepared for delivery in the classroom need less preparation time. Many instructors mention that the second time they teach a course with clickers requires much less preparation than the first time.

VENDOR SELECTION AND ADOPTION

What are some important factors to consider when choosing a particular brand of classroom response system?

This section looks at some potentially important factors to consider when deciding among competing classroom response system vendors. Various factors may be more or less important to those on a campus making adoption decisions. Technical and logistical features of these systems can vary dramatically by vendor and can change rapidly, however, so there may be important features or factors to consider that are not listed here. Those involved in making clicker adoption decisions are advised to use this section as a starting point in drafting their own lists of important factors.

Cost Factors

• What are the costs to students? How much will students have to pay for clicker hardware? Will they have to pay any ongoing fees, such as per-semester registration or licensing fees? What options will they have for selling used clickers to the vendor, a campus bookstore, or other students? Will the vendor purchase from students used clickers manufactured by other vendors?

• What are the costs to the institution? How much do receivers cost? Are there any fees for classroom response system software or fees for technical support from the vendor? What options will institutions have for selling used receivers to the vendor? Will the vendor purchase used receivers manufactured by other vendors?

• Does the vendor offer a discount to students or to the institution if an adoption or exclusivity agreement is signed? The adopting unit can typically be an entire institution or a college, school, or department within that institution, although agreements vary. Typical agreements stipulate that only the vendor's system can be centrally supported by the adopting unit's technical support staff. Other systems can be used by individual instructors provided they do not need central technical support. Some vendors discount the cost of clickers or receivers for units that sign adoption agreements; others provide free clickers or receivers or additional on-site training.

• Does the vendor partner with any textbook publishers? If so, are any discounts offered to students who purchase clickers along with textbooks from those publishers? Some publishers bundle discounted clickers with textbooks; others bundle coupons with textbooks that students can use to save money on clickers.

Hardware Factors

• What do the vendor's clickers look like? Do they have liquid crystal display (LCD) screens that provide students with additional feedback and input options? How large or small are the clickers? Are they oriented vertically (like a television remote control) or horizontally (like a computer keyboard)? What kind of batteries do the clickers use? Are they specialized batteries that students might find difficult or expensive to replace? How long does a set of batteries typically last?

• What features do the vendor's receivers have? Will they be easy for instructors to bring to a classroom and set up at the beginning of a class session? Will they be easy to install permanently in classrooms? How do the receivers connect to classroom computers? Do the receivers include LCD screens that provide information about students' responses to instructors prior to the display of results by the system's software? How many clickers can work with a single receiver? How quickly can a receiver process signals from clickers? How far away can a clicker be from the receiver while still successfully sending a signal?

• What frequencies does the system use to communicate between clickers and receivers? Does the system allow instructors to switch frequencies (usually referred to as switching channels) to avoid interference with other classroom response systems or other technologies nearby? Older systems use infrared frequencies that require line of sight between clicker and receiver and limit the number of responses that can be collected simultaneously. This means that students must aim their clickers at the receiver, so the receivers often need to be mounted near the ceilings of classrooms for all students to have clear lines of sight. The limit on the number of simultaneous responses means that multiple receivers are often required for larger classes. Newer systems use radio frequencies that do not require line of sight and allow more responses to be collected simultaneously. These advantages mean that a single receiver placed anywhere that is convenient in a classroom typically suffices.

• What warranties or return policies does the vendor offer? Are there ways to upgrade the firmware embedded within clickers and receivers without having to replace the hardware?

Software Factors

• With which operating systems (Microsoft Windows, Apple's Mac OS, Linux, and so on) does the software function? In what ways does the software function differently when running on different operating systems? Some systems have more limited features when running on Mac or Linux operating systems.

• What needs to be installed on the classroom computer in order for the system to work—only the software itself or other programs, such as Microsoft PowerPoint? Can the software be installed and run from a thumb drive instead? Can data from a class session easily be saved to a folder of the user's choice for later analysis?

Accessibility

• How easily can students with physical disabilities, including sensory impairments, use the system? For example, does the vendor make available braille clickers for students with visual impairments? Some vendors make available virtual clickers—software programs that are installed and run on laptops that enable students to use their laptops to submit responses to clicker questions. Are these programs compatible with screen readers designed for students with visual impairments? Do the frequencies used by the clickers and receivers to communicate interfere with assistive listening devices that students with auditory impairments might use? Systems that use radio frequencies are often able to change the channels that they use to communicate, making it easier to avoid conflicts with assistive listening devices.

Registration Methods

• Can students register their clickers' serial numbers using the local online course management system? If so, what is the process? Can instructors easily export class rosters from the course management system to the classroom response system? These class rosters match clicker serial numbers (entered by students through the course management system) with student names (already known to the course management system) so that the students' responses during class are identified and not anonymous. Many instructors prefer to use this registration method since it leverages the availability of existing course management systems.

• Does the system provide a way to register students' clickers during class? Some clickers with LCD screens allow students to enter their names or student identification numbers into the clickers. These data can then be submitted along with responses to clicker questions so that the responses thus provided are identified. Other systems have different methods of allowing students to register their clickers during class. These methods can make it easier to use clickers on the first day of class, since they do not require students to follow any preclass registration instructions. Instead, instructors can instruct students to follow the registration process during that first day and begin using clickers immediately.

• What other registration methods does the vendor provide? Does the vendor have a Web site where students can register their clickers and instructors can download class rosters? Does use of such a Web site require students to provide the vendor with information protected by student privacy laws such as the U.S. Family Educational Rights and Privacy Act? Does the vendor provide a Web application that offers similar functionality that can be installed on local Web servers so that student data can be maintained locally? While most vendors provide ways to register clickers through popular course management systems, not all campuses uses those systems. Having other methods of online registration can be helpful on those campuses, particularly if the vendor's in-class registration method is cumbersome or not available.

• Can clickers be used fully anonymously so that not even the instructor can identify student responses? Instructors not interested in tracking student responses and instructors wanting to ask student perspective questions about sensitive topics often desire this option. Some classroom response systems require students to register their clickers before using them, preventing the use of clickers in fully anonymous mode.

Delivery Modes

• Does the system integrate with Microsoft PowerPoint or other presentation software? If so, how does that integration work? Some systems allow instructors to enter questions and answer choices within PowerPoint or other presentation programs. These systems add interactive clicker elements to PowerPoint or other presentations, and they can feel intuitive to instructors already experienced with presentation programs. Instructors who frequently use these programs often consider this integration an important factor.

• Does the system provide a floating toolbar mode? In this mode, the classroom response system software appears as a toolbar that floats above other windows on-screen and allows instructors to initiate the collection of student responses at any time. Questions and answers can be displayed on the screen with any program (presentation programs, word processing programs, Web browsers, and so on). Screenshots are taken by the software when the collection of student responses is initiated as a way to record those questions. This mode makes it relatively easy for instructors to use specialized software to present questions during class, sometimes an important factor for instructors in fields that use disciplinary-specific notation. However, this mode often makes it difficult to designate correct answers to clicker questions before class, which can be a drawback for instructors who use indicators for correct answers during class.

• Does the system make it easy to ask questions on the fly during class? Most systems provide some kind of tool that allows instructors to collect student responses to questions not planned before class. (Floating toolbar modes inherently provide mechanisms for these questions.) Can an instructor pose a question verbally or on a chalkboard, dry erase board, or overhead transparency and collect responses on the fly? Does the system allow instructors to quickly type questions into the system during class so that these questions are captured for later analysis? If the system integrates with PowerPoint or other presentation programs, how does it integrate on-the-fly questions with existing presentations?

• Does the system provide a student-paced mode? This mode allows students to submit answers asynchronously. For example, students might be given a multiple-choice exam on paper and use their clickers to submit their answers at their own pace during class, replacing the bubble sheets often used to collect answers for these kinds of tests. Student-paced modes require clickers with LCD screens.

• Does the system provide a homework mode? This mode allows students to save to their clickers their answers to questions outside class, then submit those answers in a batch during class. This allows for rapid collection and analysis of homework questions. Homework modes require clickers with LCD screens.

• Does the system allow an instructor to use a remote control to manage the system during class? If so, can an instructor also control PowerPoint or other presentation programs using the same remote? These features allow instructors to walk around a classroom and control the classroom response system or presentation programs without having to press buttons or keys at the classroom computer. Some systems provide their own instructor remotes; others, particularly those well integrated with PowerPoint, work with standard presentation remotes.

• What options does the system provide to monitor student responses as they are collected? Most systems provide a counter or meter that displays how many students have responded at any given moment. Most systems also provide a response grid in which each cell displays a student name, student identification number, or clicker serial number. When a student's response is successfully submitted, that student's grid cell changes color or otherwise indicates that the answer has been accepted. Clickers with LCD screens usually provide this kind of feedback to students directly, so response grids are more useful with clickers lacking LCD screens. Some systems allow instructors to view the distribution of responses as they are being collected without showing students. Most systems also allow instructors to set limits on the amount of time students have to respond to a question and provide countdown timers on-screen to communicate these time limits to students.

Question Types

• How many choices does the system permit for multiple-choice questions? Do the clickers have true and false or yes and no buttons to make it easier for students to respond to these questions?

- Does the system permit the use of free-response questions? If so, are these limited to questions with numerical answers, such as 121, 6.2, and −4? If alphanumerical responses are possible, are students able to enter such responses quickly and easily? For instance, many students are efficient at entering information as they would a text message on their cell phones; an alpha-numerical entry mode that functioned similarly would be easy for these students to use.
- Does the system enable other types of questions? For instance, some systems allow students to rank a set of responses from first to last. Others allow students to respond to a multiple-choice question by selecting as many answer choices as they wish.

Result Displays

- What types of charts does the system make available for displaying results to multiple-choice questions: vertical bar charts, horizontal bar charts, pie charts, others?
- Does the system allow instructors to view individual student responses during the response collection time or after results are displayed? Some instructors like to use these features to know which students to call on during a classwide discussion. Does the system allow instructors to easily export student responses to other programs, such as spreadsheet programs, during class? Statistics instructors, for instance, might have students submit numerical data using their clickers and export these data to a spreadsheet or statistical computation program for analysis during class.
- Does the system allow the display of the results of two identical clicker questions on the same bar chart? For example, an instructor might ask the same clicker question at the beginning and the end of class, displaying both sets of results on the same bar chart at the end of class as in Figure 5.1. This display format makes clear the changes in student responses to the same clicker question over time. For instance, it would appear from the chart in Figure 5.1 that students were confused about the question initially, but most came to agree on answer C when the question was asked later. Some systems require instructors to plan these results displays before class; others allow instructors to generate them on the fly during class.

FIGURE 5.1. SAMPLE BAR CHART SHOWING PRE- AND POSTTEST RESULTS.

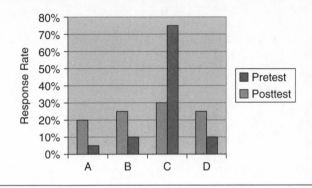

• Does the system allow the display of the results of two different clicker questions on the same bar chart? For example, an initial question might ask for students' genders. Results to a subsequent question might then be displayed as seen in Figures 5.2 or 5.3. Either type of chart can be helpful in parsing responses to a question by demographic characteristics. These charts can be useful with confidence-level questions, as seen in Figure 3.1.

• Does the system allow instructors to filter the results of one question by the responses to a previous question? For example, an initial question might ask for students' genders. Results to a subsequent question could be filtered so that only responses from

FIGURE 5.2. SAMPLE BAR CHART SHOWING RESULTS OF A CLICKER QUESTION BY DEMOGRAPHIC.

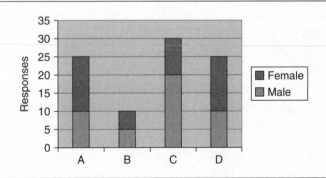

FIGURE 5.3. SAMPLE BAR CHARTS SHOWING RESULTS OF A CLICKER QUESTION BY DEMOGRAPHIC.

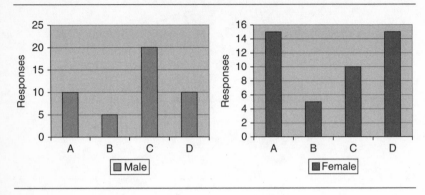

students identifying as female to the earlier question would be included in the display chart. This kind of data filtering is useful for discovering correlations in student response data, demographic or otherwise.

• Does the system allow the instructor to display a list of the students who responded first to a question? Does it allow instructors to display a list of the students who answered the most questions correctly in a class session? Does it allow students to assign themselves to teams and instructors to display a list of the highest-scoring teams? These kinds of result displays allow classroom response systems to facilitate classroom games.

• If the system enables free-response questions, how are the results of these questions displayed? Results to a numerical question might be displayed in a histogram or on a number line. Results to an alphanumerical question might list the most commonly submitted responses or display all the responses in a "word cloud" in which more commonly submitted responses are presented in correspondingly larger type sizes, as seen in the short film *Connected* produced by Abilene Christian University (2008). Since responses to free-response questions are more difficult to analyze during class, any tools the response system provides that facilitate this analysis can be important.

• Does the system allow instructors to display the results submitted thus far as responses are still being collected? Does this

display update in real time as additional responses are collected? Can the instructor view this display without showing it to students? (The discussion of lower-tech options later in this chapter offers some thoughts on why this kind of feature might be useful.)
• Does the system provide the option of displaying statistical summaries of student responses? For instance, if students are asked to respond to a question with a number between 1 and 10, some systems can show the average, standard deviation, median, and total of the student responses.

Reporting and Grading Options

• What kinds of reports can the system generate from clicker response data? Can reports be generated on a single class session? On several class sessions of the instructor's choosing? On a single student? In what formats (HTML, Microsoft Excel, Adobe PDF, and so on) can reports be generated?
• What options does the system provide instructors for assigning point values to clicker questions? Most systems allow instructors to set point values independently for correct and incorrect answers. Instructors who grade clicker questions on effort assign equal point values to correct and incorrect answers. Instructors who grade clicker questions on accuracy assign zero points to incorrect answers and some positive number of points to correct answers. Instructors who use a mix of these grading styles assign some points to incorrect answers and more points to correct ones. Different classroom response systems provide different ways to assign these points—per answer choice (so that some incorrect answers might be worth more points than others), per question (so that all correct answers to a question are worth the same number of points and all incorrect answers are worth the same), per class session (so that all questions in a class session have the same point scheme), or per course (so that all questions in an entire course have the same point scheme). The last two options can be important time-saving tools, since the first two options require instructors to assign points to every clicker question they ask.
• Does the software include an internal gradebook for tracking and scoring student responses over an entire course? If so, what features does this gradebook provide? How easy is it to use?

- Does the system allow instructors to upload grades from the classroom response system to the gradebook of the local online course management system? If so, how is this accomplished? Is the mechanism simple and efficient for instructors to use? Must every class session's clicker scores be uploaded separately, or can scores from multiple class sessions be combined before being uploaded? Many instructors who grade their clicker questions and use the gradebook feature in their course management system to communicate grades to students consider these integration features critical.
- How well does the system facilitate research into student responses to clicker questions? For instance, does the system record response times? If so, are they recorded to the nearest second or more precisely than that? If a student responds more than once to a clicker question, are all the student's responses recorded or just the final one? How accessible are the data that the system collects? Are the data kept in files with proprietary file formats, or can the data easily be exported into spreadsheet or statistical analysis programs?

Why might an academic unit (a department, college, school, or university) adopt a brand of classroom response system for use across that unit? What processes might the unit implement in order to select a brand?

As more instructors within an academic unit begin teaching with clickers, there is often pressure to adopt a single brand of clickers across the unit. This is particularly true if students are required to purchase their own clickers. If more than one brand of classroom response system is in use, then students might find themselves having to purchase two or three or more different clickers. Adopting a single brand reduces this potential cost to students. It can also help make more efficient the efforts of those who provide instructional, technical, or logistical support to instructors using clickers since these support personnel can focus their energies on learning the intricacies of a single brand of clickers.

Adoption of a single brand of clickers usually involves an agreement signed by the academic unit and the classroom response system vendor. These agreements usually stipulate that only the vendor's system can be centrally supported by the adopting unit's technical support staff, although other systems can be used by individual instructors not interested in receiving technical support. Since some vendors discount the cost of classroom response system hardware for academic units signing these agreements, adoption can provide additional savings to the academic unit or students.

Adoption can also encourage more instructors to use clickers. If, for instance, an instructor teaching a sophomore-level course knows that many of the students in that course used clickers in their first-year courses and that they all used the same brand, it becomes a little easier for that instructor to require his or her students to use clickers in that sophomore-level course since many already own the right brand of clicker.

One disadvantage of adopting a single brand of clickers for use across an academic department is that instructors who prefer to use some other brand are less able to exercise that option. An instructor using a brand of clickers not adopted by his or her school or department is not usually able to take advantage of centrally provided technical support if an adoption agreement is in place. The instructor might also encounter some resistance from students who already have purchased the brand of clickers adopted by the academic unit. This can be frustrating to experienced clicker users interested in testing new kinds of classroom response systems and to any users interested in experimenting with features available in a brand of clickers not adopted.

The process by which the decision is made to adopt a single brand of clickers and by which that brand is selected can be complex. It is often beneficial for faculty, staff, and students interested in leading this process to think carefully how to go about making these decisions: what research should be conducted, who should be involved in the process and in what ways, what kind of pilot program might be conducted, what kind of assessment and evaluation will be required once a brand of clickers has been adopted. Briggs (2008), Freeman, Bell, Comerton-Forder, Pickering, and Blayney (2007), and Twetten, Smith, Julius, and Murphy–Boyer (2007) provide descriptions of the adoption processes that several higher education institutions have implemented.

Supporting and Promoting the Use of Clickers

How can an instructor interested in using clickers for the first time get started?

There are a few typical paths instructors take when interested in experimenting with clickers in their teaching. These options are described below, but no matter what route an instructor takes, speaking with colleagues already teaching with clickers, if any are available, about pedagogical, technical, and logistical aspects of teaching with clickers on campus can be very helpful. These colleagues need not be in the same academic department. Many campuses have one or two departments where clickers are frequently used, and instructors in these departments are likely to be valuable resources for instructors in other departments getting started with clickers. Many colleges and universities have teaching and learning centers and instructional technology offices whose staff members can be valuable resources as well, particularly if classroom response systems are new to the institution. These staff members are often adept at helping instructors determine effective ways to integrate instructional technologies like classroom response systems into their teaching. Also, it is worth stating what may be obvious: instructors teaching with clickers for the first time are advised to experiment with a classroom response system before leading a class session that uses clickers. Not only will this help prevent technical problems during class, but experimenting before class begins will help instructors determine what kinds of questions and activities will work best in their courses.

One option for an instructor interested in teaching with clickers is to jump right in, asking the students in a particular course to purchase clickers at the campus bookstore and committing to use the clickers throughout that course. This option poses some risk for instructors who have not tried a more cautious option first. In particular, student course evaluations can show some negativity toward instructors who are using clickers or any other new instructional technology or teaching methodology for the first time. Course evaluations often improve over time, but initial ones can be affected by an instructor's lack of experience with clickers. It can be useful for instructors new to teaching with clickers not to grade their students' responses to clicker questions on either effort or accuracy. Leaving questions ungraded can decrease student motivation to take them seriously, but it also means that any problems, technical or otherwise, that arise do not affect student grades, and so students are likely to be a little less judgmental when problems occur. It should be noted, however, that for an instructor who has the opportunity to learn from the experiences of other instructors on campus who are experienced clicker users, jumping right in carries a little less risk.

For instructors pursuing this option, there are ways to use clickers in a course regularly and effectively that do not require an instructor to completely change his or her approach to teaching a course. For example, an instructor might add a fairly straightforward conceptual question at the beginning of a lecture as a check on student understanding of the previous lecture or perhaps an application question at the end of a lecture to assess how well students followed the lecture. Once an instructor is comfortable with these uses of clickers, he or she might add a peer instruction activity in the middle of a lecture as a way to add an interactive element to class. Starting small in the use of clickers and experimenting with other types of questions and activities over time can be a productive way to get started teaching with clickers.

Instructors who ask their students to purchase clickers at the campus bookstore must also arrange with the bookstore to make clickers available. If clickers are already in use on a campus, then bookstore staff are likely experienced with ordering and selling them. If not, then bookstore staff can still be very helpful to instructors interested in ordering clickers. Assuming an instructor has already selected a brand of classroom response system, it can be helpful to connect bookstore staff members with vendor sale representatives. These representatives are interested in making sure bookstores can easily order the right kinds of clickers. Textbook publisher representatives are also potential resources since many publishers partner with classroom response system vendors to offer discounted clickers to students who purchase textbooks from the publisher. A publisher representative might be able to arrange to have clickers or coupons for discounted clickers bundled with a textbook. One potential drawback of working through a textbook publisher, however, is that the classroom response system vendor with which the publisher has partnered may not be the vendor whose brand an instructor wishes to use in the classroom. As of this writing, there are at least half a dozen major vendors and many more smaller vendors. Some consolidation is likely to occur in time, but the marketplace is currently a crowded one.

Some instructors get started in teaching with clickers by committing to their use throughout a particular course but arrange to use a set of clickers owned by their department or another unit on campus or purchased with funds secured for this purpose instead of asking student to purchase clickers for the course. An advantage of doing so is that students need not spend money on an instructional technology of which the instructor is unsure. If technical problems or instructional challenges prevent the clickers from being used effectively in the course, then students do not get frustrated that they paid for an ineffective or unused piece of instructional technology.

This more cautious course of action is limited by the availability of a classroom response system with as many clickers as there are students in the course. Some academic departments purchase sets of clickers that instructors can check out and use in their courses. It may even be possible for an instructor to lobby his or her department to purchase such a set, particularly if multiple instructors are willing to use them. On some campuses, other units, including teaching and learning centers, instructional technology offices, and classroom media offices, have sets of clickers available for instructors to borrow. Instructors might also be able to join clicker pilot programs on some campuses in which funding is secured to purchase a set of clickers for a small group of instructors to share and evaluate. Often sets of clickers obtained in these ways only have twenty-five or thirty devices, preventing their use in larger classes, but some instructors are able to secure access to larger sets of clickers when needed.

Another disadvantage to this approach is the need to have students pick up clickers on their way into a class session and return them at the end of the class. This distribution and collection need not be time-consuming, particularly if clicker questions are left ungraded and students answer anonymously. If clicker questions are to be graded, then instructors need some way of associating each clicker in the set with an individual student in the class.

This usually means having each student pick up the same clicker, perhaps labeled with an easy-to-read identification number, at the start of class. Once an efficient system for distribution and collection has been designed, it usually works smoothly.

A third option for instructors interested in getting started with clickers is to borrow a set of clickers from one of the sources mentioned already for use in just a few class sessions. If a large enough set of clickers is available, then this can be a safe option for instructors to experiment with clickers in their classrooms, getting a feel for the technology and seeing what kinds of questions and activities might work best in their teaching context. It might be easier for instructors to borrow a set of clickers from an office on campus for a few class sessions than for an entire semester. In these cases, clickers would have to be distributed at the start of class and collected at the end of class, but these logistics are often not worrisome if limited to a few class sessions. Instructors pursuing this option might also find it helpful to discuss their intended use of clickers with a colleague who teaches with clickers or with someone from a teaching and learning center or instructional technology office and to reflect on their experiences using clickers with someone afterward. A trial run of this sort can often provide an instructor with information useful in deciding whether to implement clickers on a larger scale in subsequent courses.

What are some ways of providing initial and ongoing support to instructors using clickers?

Those interested in providing instructional, technical, or logistical support to instructors using clickers, whether they are fellow instructors or staff members in teaching and learning centers, instructional technology offices, or classroom media offices, have several options. One is to connect instructors new to using clickers with experienced users. Recruiting peer mentors in a variety of departments who are willing to talk with new clicker users can result in an effective support system.

Facilitating conversations among instructors about teaching with clickers is another effective way to provide support. These can take the form of brown bag lunch discussions, seminar-style sessions in which instructors with experience teaching with clickers share their uses of classroom response systems, or hands-on workshops in which instructors interested in teaching with clickers have the opportunity to try out the technology. As with the use of peer mentors, the peer-to-peer aspect of these kinds of gatherings can be an important aspect.

Another peer-to-peer option is to arrange for an instructor using clickers to hold an open house of sorts, inviting other instructors to visit his or her class for a day to see how clickers are used and to discuss those uses afterward. These discussions can be particularly productive given their focus on concrete examples of clicker questions and activities and student reactions observed in the host classroom. Instructors already using clickers are often able to compare and contrast their uses of clickers with those seen in the classroom visit. Framing this experience for participants can be important. If the host experiences the discussion that follows a classroom visit as a critique of his or her teaching or as merely an opportunity to receive feedback on his or her teaching, the conversation can be unproductive. Instead, the conversation should provide an opportunity for concrete discussions of the various teaching choices instructors make when using clickers, not only those choices made by the host.

More sustained peer-to-peer support can take the form of working groups consisting of instructors who meet regularly to share and receive feedback on their clicker questions and activities or to read and discuss the literature on teaching and learning with clickers and other instructional technologies. (See the discussion of improving clicker questions over time in Chapter Three for examples of these types of groups.) Providing instructors with research or salary stipends for participating in these kinds of groups can help motivate their participation. These groups can be more productive if the participants create some kind of product by the end of the working group experience: a set of clicker questions to share with colleagues in their disciplines, an article on their use of clickers to be submitted for publication in a teaching journal, or a presentation made to others on campus interested in getting started with clickers.

Some instructors can benefit from broadening their circle of clicker-using peers to instructors at other institutions. Many discipline-specific professional conferences feature workshops and presentations on teaching topics, such as the use of classroom response systems. Instructors with experience teaching with clickers might find it useful to give a talk about their experiences at one of these conferences. Conferences on teaching and learning in higher education that draw instructors from a variety of disciplines are also potential venues for cross-campus discussions about teaching with clickers. Instructors using clickers might be interested in giving talks at these conferences or in attending and hearing how colleagues at other institutions use these systems.

Sometimes instructors using clickers are less interested in talking with their peers than they are in obtaining support to resolve particular technical or instructional issues. Providing instructors with easy access to support can be very helpful, particularly since these requests for assistance are often time sensitive. If instructors know whom to call when they have a question or problem about teaching with clickers, they are more likely to seek out that help and resolve their difficulty. Thus, one-on-one consultations about both technical and instructional issues can provide a useful avenue of support for instructors.

Yaoling Wang, an instructional technology consultant at Iowa State University, has offered on-the-spot technical support to instructors using clickers by volunteering to attend their classes at the beginning of the semester to be on hand in case of technical problems. Yang says that her presence often helped instructors feel more confident using clickers for the first time since they knew she was available to help. She also says that sitting in these classrooms provided her with useful insights into challenges and opportunities in teaching with clickers. These insights enabled her to provide instructors with more meaningful support around instructional and pedagogical aspects of teaching with clickers.

Instructors teaching with clickers can benefit from assistance in gathering useful feedback from their students. Instead of waiting until the end of a semester to gather this feedback from standard student course evaluations, it can often be helpful to seek out this information in the middle of the semester. This provides enough time for both students and instructor to become accustomed to using clickers but is early enough in the semester so that the instructor can, if necessary, make changes to his or her instructional practice in response to the feedback. There are many student surveys used by instructors at different kinds of institutions in the literature on teaching with clickers. Graham, Tripp, Seawright, and Joeckel (2007), Nagy-Shadman and Desrochers (2008), and Trees and Jackson (2007) describe useful and interesting student surveys that might serve as models for instructors seeking midsemester feedback.

How might instructors who have used clickers successfully encourage their colleagues to try teaching with clickers?

Following are just a few ideas for activities that instructors might use to interest their colleagues in experimenting with clickers.

Many campuses host workshops featuring instructors who share their experiences teaching with clickers. Instructors often appreciate hearing from their peers and colleagues about their teaching experiences. Workshops can be useful opportunities for instructors involved in working groups to share their work with the campus. Workshops featuring instructors willing to serve as peer mentors for other instructors new to teaching with clickers can be particularly useful, since they help connect instructors interesting in trying clickers with peers interested in assisting them.

Workshops can be useful, but their success depends on whether instructors who are not already using clickers will take time out of their day to attend a workshop. Instructors not already familiar with clickers might not be inclined to do so. Another option is to model the use of clickers at faculty meetings, faculty and teaching assistant orientations, and other events where instructors are present. Many instructors need only see clickers in action once before they start realizing some of the ways clickers can be useful in their courses. As long as their experience using clickers at one of these events is a positive one, this method can interest instructors in the technology. It is often helpful to let instructors attending such an event know with whom they can speak if they are interested in trying out clickers in their courses. This plants the idea that clickers might play a role in their teaching, and it provides them with a convenient first step for getting started experimenting with clickers.

Another option is to invite a colleague to one's class to see clickers in action. Once instructors see clickers in use, they often start thinking about applications to their own classrooms. Having a colleague attend a class session to see how clickers are used can make the technology and its application in the classroom more concrete. At many campuses, however, instructors do not visit each other's classrooms regularly except for the purpose of evaluating a colleague as part of a tenure or promotion decision. Being invited to visit a colleague's class in order to have a stimulating conversation about teaching might come as a surprise to some instructors. Teaching need not be a private act, however; it is often more effective and more enjoyable when approached as a community endeavor.

Because one option for getting started teaching with clickers is to borrow a set of clickers for use in a few class sessions, a department, teaching and learning center, instructional technology office, classroom media office, or an individual instructor with the right funding might purchase a set of clickers to lend to instructors for this purpose. It can be helpful to meet with an instructor before he or she borrows a set to discuss options for facilitating questions in the classroom and to meet with him or her afterward to discuss the experience.

Whatever the method for interesting one's colleagues in clickers, it is important to remember that how an instructor uses clickers depends on his or her teaching context: the nature of the course, the nature of the students, and even the physical aspects of the classroom. The ways in which one instructor uses clickers might not work well for another instructor. When discussing clickers with colleagues, it can be helpful to start the conversation by asking about their teaching. Are they interested in finding out how well their students understand their lectures on a more regular basis? Are they interested in adding interactivity to their class sessions? Are they interested in administering quizzes more efficiently? There are a variety of reasons instructors might be interested in using clickers. Finding out what those reasons are can be a useful first step in interesting colleagues in using clickers.

Bruff (2007), Deal (2007), and Zhu (2007) provide brief introductions to teaching with clickers that can be shared with colleagues who prefer reading about new teaching methods. Introductions such as these make useful handouts at workshops about teaching with clickers.

LOW-TECH OPTIONS

What are some low-tech assessment methods that are similar to classroom response systems? What advantages do clickers have over these methods?

Hand-Raising Method. A common method for having students respond to a multiple-choice question during class is to ask for a show of hands. Suppose a question has three answer choices: A, B, and C. The instructor first poses the question and gives students time to think about and commit to their answers. Then the instructor asks all the students who selected answer A to raise their hands, then the students who selected answer B, then the students who selected answer C.

The hand-raising method has several advantages. Asking students to respond to a question can focus their attention during class, and asking for a show of hands provides all students with a way to respond to a question. This method is a fast way for instructors to gauge their students' understanding or perspectives on an issue. It also allows students to see what their peers think, which can help students learn to appreciate diversity of thought and let students know they are not alone in their thinking. Furthermore, this method does not require any technology, which makes it cost efficient and reliable.

The fact that students see each other's responses is a significant drawback to this method. Since student responses are not anonymous when this method is used, some students can be hesitant to answer a hand-raising question honestly. Some worry about having a minority perspective on an issue; others worry about answering a question incorrectly in front of their peers. Freeman, Blayney, and Ginns (2006) provide evidence that students' willingness to respond to an in-class question decreases when they are not allowed to do so anonymously.

The hand-raising method also makes it fairly easy for a student to change his or her answer to a question in response to how classmates vote. This makes it easier for students to take questions less seriously and harder for instructors to use the results of these questions in making classroom decisions. Some classroom response systems can be used to demonstrate that students change their responses to a hand-raising question after they see how others respond.

Adam Rich, who teaches an anatomy and physiology course at the State University of New York at Brockport, and Weston Dripps, who teaches earth and environmental courses at Furman University, use a classroom response system that permits the distribution of responses to be shown to students during the collection of these responses. This bar chart changes in real time to reflect the votes as they are cast. Neither instructor uses this feature, but both have inadvertently turned it on during class sessions. Each noted that once one of the answer choices became a little more popular than the others, the students converged on that answer almost completely. They took these incidents as evidence that when students know how their classmates are voting, peer pressure can trump any efforts to have students thoughtfully consider the question at hand. Bunce, VandenPlas, and Havanki (2006) report a similar phenomenon. It is possible that this effect happens regularly with the hand-raising method of classroom assessment.

The hand-raising method also makes it difficult to record student responses to a question. (One could, in theory, take a few digital pictures of a class during the show of hands and analyze those pictures later to determine each student's response. This is not very practical, however.) This means that students cannot easily be held accountable for their answers, particularly in large classes. It also means that this method is not useful for graded quiz or exam questions, and it does not generate useful data on student learning for classroom research purposes.

Response Cards. Another alternative to the use of a classroom response system is having students respond to multiple-choice questions with response cards. A set of response cards might consist of five cards, each labeled with an answer choice (A, B, C, D, and E, for instance). Each card might be white on the blank side and color-coded on the side with the answer choices (for example, A on a blue background, B on a red background, and so on). Thus, when students hold up their cards to respond to the question, the instructor can quickly judge the distribution of student responses by the colors visible from the front of the classroom. Most students, however, see only the backs of the cards of the students in front of them. Since these backs are all identical, students are not generally aware of their peers' responses. This method takes some preparation, since students must create or be supplied with sets of response cards. A deck of playing cards can work well for questions with four answer choices: red face cards for A, red numbered cards for B, black face cards for C, and black numbered cards for D.

Some instructors distribute dry erase boards and markers to their students instead of response cards. Students then write their answer choices on their dry erase boards and display them for the instructor to respond to a question. The use of color-coded markers (blue for A, red for B, and so on) can help instructors scan responses quickly. Dry erase boards can also be used to have students respond to a question with a word or phrase, although these responses are harder for instructors to scan quickly, especially in a large room. Another option is to have students hold their fingers in front of their chests to indicate their responses: one finger for answer A, two fingers for answer B, and so on (Slater, 2005). This method works similarly to the response card method but requires no preparation. The finger-to-chest method, however, can make it more difficult for instructors to get a sense of the distribution of answers.

These methods can be less costly and less susceptible to failure than the use of clickers. Another advantage is that they make it easy for instructors to see the responses of individual students. This allows an instructor to say, for instance, "John, I see you chose answer B. Would you mind explaining to the class why you selected that answer?" Of course, calling on a student in this fashion removes the anonymity he or she otherwise would enjoy under this method, which can be problematic in some contexts. (Some classroom response systems also make it fairly easy for instructors to see the responses of individual students.)

Like the use of classroom response systems and the hand-raising method, response card methods can increase student participation since all students are asked to respond to a question. These methods also help to focus students' attention during class and engage them with questions by asking them to commit to their answers by signifying those answers to the instructor.

Response card methods also provide instructors with information on student learning and student perspectives that can inform on-the-spot teaching decisions.

An advantage that response card methods have over the hand-raising method is that they make it more difficult for students to know how their peers respond to a question, encouraging them to respond to questions independently and allowing them to respond more anonymously. In theory, only the instructor can see the students' responses, although in practice, some students are able to see their neighbors' responses. In fact, there is some evidence that response card methods do not provide more independent and anonymous responses than the hand-raising method. In a study of an introductory psychology course, Stowell and Nelson (2007) compared student performance on quiz questions asked during a lecture using three different response methods—hand raising, response cards, and clickers—with their performance on quiz questions asked after a lecture. Although the students who responded during lecture with clickers scored somewhat lower on the postlecture quiz than on the in-lecture questions, the students who responded using the hand-raising and response card methods scored much lower on the postlecture quiz. The researchers' conclusion was that students answered clicker questions during class more honestly than they did using the hand-raising or response card methods. Both of the latter methods enabled students to see their peers' responses, change their own response, and, as a result, answer more questions correctly during class. When the students were required to answer on their own during the postlecture quiz, they did not perform nearly so well. It is possible that the responses an instructor sees when using response card methods may lead the instructor to believe that more students understand a question than is really the case.

Recent investigations by Marcie Desrochers and Andrew Knapp of the State University of New York at Brockport psychology department indicate that variations on the response card method described here might avoid this issue. They compared student performance on in-class questions between two groups of students: those who responded to multiple-choice questions with clickers and those who responded to fill-in-the-blank questions by writing responses on index cards and showing them to the instructor. Students in the former group answered more questions correctly during class than students in the latter group, but both groups scored similarly on a postpresentation quiz. Students in a third group who did not respond to any questions during the presentation performed more poorly on the postpresentation quiz than the students who responded by either of the two response methods. One could argue from these results that having students respond to questions during class by some method is better than not having them respond at all, which is consistent with research exploring the impact of teaching strategies that feature active learning methods (Hake, 1998). One could also argue that having students write responses to fill-in-the-blank questions on index cards makes it more difficult for them to copy each other's answers than usual response card and dry erase board methods. The fact that students who responded using index cards scored as well on the postpresentation quiz as students who responded using clickers might indicate that clickers do not offer much advantage in terms of short-term student learning over other response methods. However, since a video presentation was used, the responses of the students did not affect the instruction they received. It is possible that when results from clicker questions are used to facilitate agile teaching, clickers enable greater learning gains than other response methods. More research investigating these issues is needed.

One disadvantage that response card methods have is that the distribution of responses is not visible to the students, limiting the impact of any communication of the results to the students. This means, for instance, that students with minority perspectives might not be as willing to speak up in front of their peers since they are not as aware of how many of their classmates agree with them. This also means that students are less aware of how well they understand a content question in relation to their peers. Another disadvantage to the use of response card methods is that student responses are not recorded for later use. As a result, students are less accountable for their responses, which can limit their participation and engagement. For example, Holly Bender, who teaches courses in veterinary medicine at Iowa State University, used response cards in her courses for several semesters. She found that the response cards provided useful feedback on her students' learning, but since she could not count their answers toward their grades, many students did not engage in the process. She now uses clickers, which allow her to hold students accountable for class participation, which encourages more of them to participate.

Choral Response. Another response method that features some of the benefits of the use of clickers is the use of choral response, which Marcie Desrochers of the State University of New York at Brockport sometimes employs. In this method, an instructor poses a multiple-choice or free-response question and gives students time to think about and commit to their responses. Then students are instructed to state their responses verbally at the same time. Desrochers finds that she can make some sense of her students' responses using this method, determining if there is disagreement or consensus and assessing her students' confidence by the volume of their responses.

Choral response offers many of the advantages of other response methods. Students are asked to think and answer questions independently, and the simultaneous verbal nature of the responses can make it difficult for them to change their responses on learning their peers' responses. Students are asked to commit to answers, which can increase their engagement with the question and any discussion of its answer. Since both students and instructors are able to make some sense of the distribution of responses, instructors can use the responses to make on-the-spot teaching decisions and students can learn a little about their peers' perspectives.

The difficulty of determining the distribution of responses with choral response limits its use in providing feedback. Also, verbal answers are less anonymous than answers submitted by clickers or response card methods since students are often able to hear the responses of students sitting nearby. This method does not scale up well to large classes since the more students who respond, the harder it can be to determine anything about the distribution of responses. In addition, students are even less accountable for their answers when responding verbally than when responding using any of the other methods described here. It is easy for a student who remains silent to be undetected by an instructor, and there is no record of individual student responses. This can lead to decreased student participation and engagement with the question-and-answer process. It also means that choral response is not helpful for graded quizzes or gathering data on student learning. Choral response can be fun, however, when used as an occasional alternative to other response methods.

Written Responses. A final option for instructors considering low-tech alternatives to clickers is to have students write their answers to a multiple-choice or free-response question on slips of paper and pass those slips of paper to their instructor. The instructor reads a sample of the responses aloud to the class. If students are asked to write their names on these slips of paper, this method can be used to hold students accountable for their answers, an advantage of this method over the hand-raising, response card, and choral response methods. This can increase student participation and engagement and also means that this method can be used for graded work and gathering data on student learning in support of classroom research. This method allows student responses to be somewhat anonymous and independent since students are often able to prevent their neighbors from seeing their responses as they write them.

One disadvantage of this method is that it can take some time to collect and read student responses. Another is that the method makes it difficult for instructors to get a sense of all their students' responses, limiting its use in agile teaching. Instructors are generally limited to reading responses silently or aloud one at a time and looking for patterns as they do so. It is also limited in providing students with insight into what their peers think because only responses that are read aloud by the instructor are heard by other students. This method does not scale up well either, since the larger the class, the smaller the percentage of student responses that can be read aloud.

This method is perhaps most useful when instructors want to share with the class a random sample of student responses to free-response questions. Since students are asked to submit their answers in writing, they are more likely to answer independently, which can help them think more deeply about the question at hand and help generate a wider variety of responses than a question answered verbally would. Although only a portion of student responses could be used during the class session, all responses could be analyzed after class for use in subsequent classes.

Summary. Several low-tech methods for requesting responses from students during class approximate the use of a classroom response system. None of the methods described here offers all of the benefits of the use of clickers, however. The hand-raising, response card, and choral response methods lack the ability to hold students accountable for their responses, which makes it easier for students to disengage from the question-and-answer process, and they can make it difficult to have students respond anonymously and independently. Having students submit answers on slips of paper can hold students accountable for their answers and can make it easier to have students respond anonymously and independently. However, this method is time-consuming, limited in the feedback it provides, and does not scale up well to large courses.

High-Tech Options

Laptops and cell phones can sometimes function as part of classroom response systems. Because these high-tech options are likely to change rapidly in the next few years, readers interested in exploring classroom response systems that use laptops, cell phones, or other devices are advised to use the discussion here as a starting point for their investigations.

How can student laptops be used as part of classroom response systems?

As of this writing, there are two primary ways in which student laptops are sometimes used as part of classroom response systems. One method is through the use of software programs made available by response system vendors that can be installed on laptops to allow them to function as clickers. Typically with these programs, instructors let their students know the Internet protocol (IP) address of their classroom computer. Students then run virtual clicker programs on their laptops, sending responses to the

IP address provided by their instructors. Responses submitted by both clickers and laptops are then combined on the instructor's classroom computer. Some students in the class respond with clickers, while others respond using their laptops and a wired or wireless Internet connection. These systems also allow students to participate in clicker questions at a distance. The instructor and some students with clickers can be in one location, and other students using laptops can be in another location, participating through Web conferencing or videoconferencing.

Other laptop-based classroom response systems are designed to function without handheld clickers. Although virtual clicker programs typically offer students the same response options as clickers, laptop-only systems often offer more flexible free-response options, sometimes including the ability for students to submit images and files in response to questions. These systems require all students to have laptops with Internet connectivity. Some of these programs are Web based and thus do not require students to install programs on their laptops.

Many of the classroom response systems that incorporate laptops in either of the two ways described make it easier for students to respond to free-response questions than traditional clicker systems do, in part because most allow students to type their answers using their laptop keyboard. Using laptops also leverages an existing resource for many students: their laptops. Students need not purchase dedicated devices (clickers) that cannot be used for other functions. Also, since many instructors report students using laptops to distract themselves during class (surfing the Web, checking their e-mail, and so on), using laptops as response devices gives them something productive to do with their computers during class. Furthermore, once students are using laptops actively as response devices, they might also use them productively in other ways, such as locating information relevant to class discussions on the Internet, taking notes during class, or experimenting with online simulations of science and other experiments. In addition, some of the more robust laptop-based classroom response systems allow other useful classroom communications, such as file sharing among instructor and students, homework submission, displaying student work on the classroom projector, and integrating with online course management systems.

A disadvantage of using laptops with Internet connectivity during class as response devices is that students might use those laptops for less productive purposes. Using laptops as response devices during class also requires a classroom with enough power outlets and sufficient Internet connectivity. Some students might not appreciate having to bring their laptops to class regularly. Furthermore, classroom response system software can sometimes function differently on different operating systems. Web-based software sometimes relies on students using certain Web browsers. Unless students all use identical laptops, operating systems, and Web browsers, laptop-based systems can run the risk of incompatibility and trouble-shooting issues. Using dedicated clicker devices minimizes this risk.

How can student cell phones be used as part of classroom response systems?

One way in which student cell phones might be used as response devices is that so-called smart phones—cell phones with Internet connectivity using wireless or cellular networks—can sometimes run response system programs similar to those used on laptops, particularly ones that are Web based. This allows students with these phones to use them in classroom response systems as if the smart phones were small, very portable laptops. Given the increasing power and prevalence of smart phones, there is interest in developing classroom response systems that make use of these devices (Abilene Christian University, 2008).

Although an increasing number of student cell phones have Internet connectivity, even more have text-messaging capabilities. Another way of using cell phones as response devices leverages these capabilities by having students text their responses to questions to an instructor's or a teaching assistant's cell phone. (See the description of Charlene Harkins's use of text messaging as a backchannel by which students submitted questions during her lectures in Chapter Three for an example of a text-messaging-based classroom response system.) Potentially more useful are systems that allow students to text their responses to a service that provides instructors with results they can display on their classroom computer. Scornavacca and Marshall (2007) and Cheung (2008) describe such systems.

Given how quickly many students can type on a cell phone using the various methods by which cell phones allow data entry, cell phones can allow students to respond more quickly to free-response questions than clickers often do. Individual students are more likely to have cell phones than laptops, so using cell phones as response devices leverages a widespread existing resource. Students are not likely to forget to bring their cell phone to class given how often they usually use their phones during the day, nor are they likely to mind bringing the phone to class as much as they might mind bringing a laptop. Smart phones can also be used in other productive ways during class, similar to the productive ways in which laptops can be used. Furthermore, cell phones typically require recharging less frequently than laptops, reducing the need for power outlets in the classroom.

Nevertheless, students can find cell phones even more distracting than laptops during class, particularly cell phones with the Internet connectivity or text-messaging capabilities necessary for their use as response devices. Using cell phones with wireless Internet connectivity as response devices requires a classroom with sufficient Internet connectivity to support that use. Having students submit responses to questions by text messaging requires them to have text-messaging service plans, which can be expensive. Systems that rely on text messaging or cellular Internet connectivity also require students to have reliable cell phone access to nearby cellular towers.

CHAPTER SIX

WHY USE CLICKERS?

Instructors teach with classroom response systems for a variety of reasons. Some of the benefits of clickers, such as the ability to collect student feedback rapidly, are difficult to achieve in large courses without classroom response systems. Other benefits, such as the ability for students to respond anonymously to questions, are relevant regardless of the number of students in a course. This conclusion discusses reasons to teach with clickers, highlighting the unique capabilities of these response systems to enable classroom experiences that are difficult to achieve without clickers and to enhance other teaching methods that can be used with or without clickers.

INCREASED STUDENT PARTICIPATION

A classroom response system can be used to increase student participation during class in several ways, one of which is increasing the percentage of students who participate during class. Clickers provide each student with a chance to respond to a question, including shy students who might not volunteer an answer verbally during class. Charlene Harkins of the University of Minnesota at Duluth finds that clickers do a good job of engaging students in her three-hundred-student nutrition course who are not usually active participants but are willing to engage with the course under the right conditions. Also, since classroom response systems allow instructors to monitor the number of responses to a clicker question as students respond, instructors can keep collecting responses until most or all students have had a chance to respond. This can increase the participation of students who are not typically able to compose a response quickly enough to participate in a classwide discussion. Some students are not able to volunteer answers during class simply due to time constraints; there are only so many opportunities for students to respond during any given class session. Clickers give these students a voice as well. Furthermore, as Thomas Palmeri of Vanderbilt University points out, using a classroom response system encourages his psychology students to ask more questions of him during and after class. He says that there is something about pressing a button on a clicker that lowers the barrier between students and instructor.

Since classroom response systems can be used to identify the responses of individual students, they allow instructors to hold students accountable for their participation in class sessions, which also increases student participation. Particularly in large classes, students can often avoid participation and engagement because it is difficult for their instructors to know who they are and how they are contributing during any particular class session. Clickers allow instructors to hold students accountable for their contributions and participation, particularly when responses are factored into their grades. Adam Rich of the State University of New York at Brockport often begins class with two quick clicker questions, which motivates his students to arrive on time. He also finds that his students' attendance improves when he uses clickers: attendance rates in his 170-student anatomy and physiology course increased from 60 percent to 90 percent when he began using clickers. Elizabeth Cullingford of the University of Texas at Austin finds useful the record of student attendance her classroom response system generates. When students ask her why they are doing poorly in her 250-student literature course, she can see how often they skip classes and respond accordingly. Corly Brooke of Iowa State University points out that although some of the students in her human development course do not engage during class by answering clicker questions, she feels that more students would be disengaged without them.

Classroom response systems also allow students to respond to questions without their peers knowing how they respond. This anonymity can make it easier for students to express minority perspectives and for students to respond to questions without worrying about answering incorrectly in front of their peers. Philippa

Levine of the University of Southern California finds that students in her 180-student history course on the evolution debates are often hesitant to speak up during class for this reason. She notes that clickers offer her students the chance to express themselves confidentially, which encourages them to state their true opinions and beliefs about controversial topics. In smaller courses, the anonymity that clickers provide can be the most important feature of classroom response systems. As mentioned in Chapter Four, Teresa Cosby uses clickers in her upper-level political science seminar courses at Furman University. She believes that some of her students, even in this small class setting, are hesitant to speak up during class out of fear of offending her, an African American woman, or other students on particularly sensitive topics. Since Cosby does not track individual student responses, clickers allow these students to respond anonymously and perhaps more honestly.

INCREASED STUDENT ENGAGEMENT

Clickers provide each student a chance to think about and respond to a question before hearing other students' answers. This opportunity for independent thinking can engage students more fully with a question by encouraging students who might typically wait to hear their peers' responses before seriously considering a question to think about a question on their own. It also can prepare students to engage in subsequent small-group and classwide discussions by giving them time to collect their thoughts about a question before sharing them publicly. Giving students the chance to respond to a question before seeing others' responses can also minimize the effect of peer pressure, which in turn can foster more diverse perspectives among students. Students who know that a particular response is an unpopular one might not consider it as seriously as other responses. Using clickers to collect responses encourages students to consider all possibilities before selecting one.

Students are usually more engaged with a task when they are asked to produce a deliverable—an outcome, result, or product that demonstrates their learning. Clickers allow instructors to request small deliverables (the responses students submit by pressing buttons on their clickers) several times in a class session, helping students focus on and engage in learning activities, such as peer instruction or classwide discussions. Knowing that a deliverable may at any time be requested from students can help students maintain attention and engagement during a class session. Also, the fact that the deliverable is a kinesthetic activity, involving movement and tactile sensation, can engage students who respond well to such activities.

Rafael Gely finds that clicker questions help keep students engaged in the class discussion in his law courses at the University of Cincinnati. Like many other law school instructors, Gely uses a form of the Socratic method in his teaching practice, calling on student volunteers during class and questioning those volunteers in order to explore particular issues. The length of one of these interchanges varies from a few minutes to an entire class session with a single student. Gely believes that focusing on a single student for a long time period can decrease other students' motivation to stay engaged with the discussion. He finds that using clickers helps keep all students engaged, since they know these discussions are frequently followed by clicker questions. Gely discusses other reasons for using clickers in his law courses in Caron and Gely (2004).

A student who responds to a clicker question makes a commitment to that answer. The simple act of pressing a button on a clicker can encourage students to take ownership of their responses to a question even when a participation or quiz grade is not on the line. This commitment can motivate them to want to know if they answered the question correctly, to know their peers' thoughts on the question, and to hear what their instructor has to say about it. Bill Hill finds this to be true in his psychology courses at Kennesaw State University. His students report on course feedback surveys that the use of clickers leads them to want to defend their responses during small-group and classwide discussion. Hill says that this is similar to the phenomenon of students questioning his grading of a missed test item; they have committed to their answer and want to defend it. The use of a classroom response system can generate this effect several times in a class session.

Classroom response systems also allow instructors to share the results of clicker questions with students, and this sharing can also help to engage students. For example, the results of a clicker question can show students that their peers have different perspectives and experiences than they do. This can encourage students to want to hear from students with different perspectives and to take those perspectives more seriously when they learn they are held by many of their peers. This can help justify to students the use of class time to explore these perspectives. The results of clicker questions can also show students that they are not alone in their perspectives. This can encourage students with minority perspectives to share them publicly.

The results of student perspective questions can have a significant impact on students' lives. Resa Walch and Amanda Tapler of Elon University asked the students in their course on contemporary issues in wellness to engage in projects in which they tried to change their own behavior regarding some wellness issue. One student saw that his drinking habits were far riskier than those of his peers in the results of a clicker question early in the course, and this motivated him to change his drinking habits for his project. Walch and Tapler felt that he was successful in part because he found the clicker data so persuasive.

When instructors share the results of clicker questions with correct and incorrect answers, these results can let students know how well their peers understand course material. Knowing that many of their classmates answered a question incorrectly can help students see the difficulty of a question and want to listen to and understand an explanation of the correct answer. This can also encourage those who do not understand a topic to speak up and ask a question. Many instructors find that students are motivated by finding out how well they understand a topic in comparison to their peers. Seeing the results of the question is essential for this.

Brian Augustine says this is true in his chemistry courses at James Madison University. He finds that a student who is wrong about a question and knows that a number of classmates were similarly wrong does not feel as bad about missing the question. The student is also more likely to listen when Augustine tells the students that a topic is worth studying for the exam and more likely to get help during his office hours. A student who is wrong about a question and knows that he or she is in the distinct minority is made keenly aware of the need to work harder to catch up with others. Thomas Benzing, who teaches a course on environmental issues in science at James Madison University, finds that results that indicate that a question is difficult for a number of students can also show students who answer the question correctly that spending class time to discuss the question is worthwhile.

Also, when the same or similar clicker questions are asked before and after a learning activity such as peer instruction or a classwide discussion, changes in the results of these questions can demonstrate to students the value and impact of the learning activity. Often students work hard during that learning activity in the hopes of seeing improved or different results on the postactivity clicker question.

Classroom response systems can also be used to engage students by making class a little more fun. Systems that track the fastest responders to questions and allow team activities can be used to conduct classroom games, as described in Chapter Two. Instructors can also add some drama to class as they reveal the results of questions, particularly if the results show split decisions or high degrees of consensus about incorrect answers. Although students do not necessarily need to have fun during class in order to learn, a little fun can enliven the classroom atmosphere. Kristen Hessler sometimes includes a few fun trivia questions as warm-up clicker questions in her philosophy courses at the State University of New York at Albany. She finds that many of her students get excited about getting these questions correct and that this friendly, competitive spirit can help keep students engaged.

FREQUENT FEEDBACK ON STUDENT LEARNING

Clickers enable instructors to collect information on student learning from all students in a classroom quickly, easily, and simultaneously. Furthermore, classroom response systems automatically summarize this information and report this summary to instructors and students in an easy-to-read bar chart. This means that quick formative assessment of student learning can be conducted several times in a single session. Instructors and students need not wait for weekly essays or homework assignments or less frequent tests and papers to find out what students do and do not understand.

The information on student learning provided by clickers can be used by instructors to modify their lesson plans during class to respond to immediate student learning needs. For example, if the clicker results indicate students understand a particular topic, instructors can move along to the next topic. If not, then more time can be spent on the topic using lecture, small-group or classwide discussion, or further clicker questions. This kind of agile teaching can be difficult to implement without clickers, particularly in large courses.

Formative assessment not only provides instructors with useful information about student learning, it also lets students know what they understand and do not understand. Since clickers can provide this information several times during a class session, they allow students to have a better sense of how well they understand material during a class session while they are able to ask questions of their instructors and their peers. Students do not have to leave such a class session wondering if they really understand the material.

Students who miss clicker questions in Karina Kline-Gabel's Spanish courses at James Madison University are often the ones who ask questions during class. Missing a question motivates them to want to get the next one correct, so they are more engaged in the discussion. The standard practice in law courses taught by Rafael Gely at the University of Cincinnati is to have a single assessment in each course: a final exam. Gely finds that first-year students have some trouble adapting to this practice from undergraduate course work in which they are typically assessed more frequently. By asking clicker questions with correct answers and grading students on their accuracy, he helps them make this transition. They appreciate getting a sense of how well they are understanding the material, as does he.

Use of a classroom response system can also greatly increase the speed and efficiency with which instructors collect, grade, and record student performance on quizzes and tests. Instructors can review quizzes and tests immediately following their completion, while the quiz questions are still fresh in the students' minds, focusing on the questions most missed by students and on incorrect answer choices most selected by students.

Clickers can provide useful feedback on student learning within a class session, but they can also help instructors make sense of student learning on longer timescales. Since classroom response systems record each student's response to each question, they provide data on student learning that can be mined to uncover patterns in student learning after individual class sessions or after a course has ended. These patterns can help instructors better understand what students learn, what they have trouble learning, and even how they learn, useful information for designing subsequent learning experiences. Weston Dripps of Furman University uses the results of his clicker questions to inform the exam questions he uses in his earth sciences courses. Knowing that students struggled with a certain topic is helpful in constructing an exam that assess them well.

Anthony Crider of Elon University has used clickers to assess his teaching methods over time in his astronomy courses. As described in Chapter Three, he asks his students, "Do you think United States astronauts landed on the moon?" several times during a unit exploring the moon landing. The first time he showed his students a documentary arguing that the moon landing was a hoax, the results of this clicker question showed him that many students were swayed by the documentary. He then had his students review a few Web sites that rebutted the documentary, but when he asked his clicker question again, he discovered that relatively few students were convinced by those sites. The next time he taught the course, he had his students complete projects about the moon landing, but his clicker question showed him that that process did not convince his students sufficiently either. The next time, he used *National Geographic* and other videos to rebut the documentary, and the results of his clicker question showed that this method made a big difference in student opinion. Also useful was giving students a series of questions to explore using Web searches during the viewing of the documentary. These questions asked students to find information about the people interviewed in the documentary, many of whom are not experts. This activity helped students think more critically about the documentary as they watched it, and fewer students were swayed by the documentary. The data provided by his classroom response system allowed Crider to refine his instructional methods each time he taught his course.

FINAL SUGGESTIONS

The sixteen suggestions that follow for teaching with classroom response systems are drawn from the previous chapters. They are intended to help instructors with or without experience teaching with clickers make more intentional choices when using clickers—choices that help them teach more effectively and lead to enhanced student learning.

1. Consider the following questions when drafting clicker questions:

   - What student learning goals do I have for the question?
   - What do I hope to learn about my students by asking this question?
   - What will my students learn about each other when they see the results of this question?
   - How might this question be used to engage students with course content in small-group or classwide discussions or by creating a time for telling?
   - What distribution of responses do I expect to see from my students?
   - What might I do if the actual distribution turns out very differently?

2. Look for answer choices for potential clicker questions in student responses to open-ended questions, ones asked on assignments in previous courses, on homework questions, or during class. This can lead to answer choices that better match common student misconceptions and perspectives.

3. Use a variety of types of clicker questions. Some courses lend themselves to particular types of questions, of course, but experimenting with different kinds of questions (application questions, critical thinking questions, student perspective questions, monitoring questions) can help instructors use clickers in ways that engage students and meet course learning goals.

4. Experiment with asking on-the-fly clicker questions—ones that are not planned before class. Many classroom response systems make asking such questions possible. Often a classwide discussion leads to spontaneous clicker questions; other times

rhetorical questions can be turned into productive clicker questions. Either way, asking such questions is one avenue for practicing agile teaching.

5. Use clickers for purposes other than quizzes and taking attendance. Although clickers can make these activities more time efficient, students often prefer to see them used in ways that are more directly connected to their learning. Reviewing the results of a quiz immediately after administering it is one way to do so. Using clickers to engage students in small-group and classwide discussions and to offer students frequent feedback on their learning is also effective.

6. Use clickers in smaller courses, particularly those that focus on sensitive or controversial topics. The anonymity that classroom response systems provide students can be important in helping them answer questions about tough topics honestly.

7. Have students respond to clicker questions several times throughout a class session. Although questions at the beginning and end of class sessions can serve particular and useful functions, questions asked every ten to fifteen minutes can help focus students' attention throughout the class.

8. For some questions, have students think of their answers before showing them the answer choices. Since generating an answer is often more challenging than selecting an answer from a given set of possibilities, this can help make clicker questions more challenging. Also, hearing from students who generate answers not listed can help you learn about your students.

9. Have students respond to a clicker question individually before discussing the question in small groups. This leverages a classroom response system's ability to allow all students a chance to think about a question independently of their peers.

10. Be strategic about showing students the results of a clicker question. If most students choose the same answer to a question with correct and incorrect answers, showing students such results might lead them to assume that the popular answer is the correct one and thus decrease their interest in discussing the question further. If students are split among more than

one answer choice, however, showing students such results can help generate small-group and classwide discussion.

11. For similar reasons, choose carefully when to indicate to students the correct answer to a clicker question. Once some students know the correct answer, they are likely to be less interested in further discussion of it, perhaps incorrectly assuming that knowing the answer means they understand the topic fully.

12. When reviewing a clicker question with students, spend at least some time on each of the answer choices—right and wrong ones. Students often appreciate hearing their instructor's perspective on the answer choices they selected, even when they know those choices are incorrect.

13. When reviewing a clicker question with students, have them share their reasons for their answers. Not only does this shift students' focus away from getting questions right or wrong and toward thinking critically, but it also provides useful insights into students' thinking.

14. When students find a question difficult, have them reengage with it through small-group or classwide discussion and then revote. Giving students multiple opportunities to answer a question while providing them with feedback mechanisms along the way can help them make sense of course material.

15. Immediately after class, take a few notes about how particular clicker questions played out during class. A little reflection right after class can help in refining and improving clicker questions over time.

16. Find other instructors who teach with classroom response systems and share experiences. Too often teaching is a private act, one instructors do not discuss with their colleagues. However, such discussions are often very useful in helping instructors teach more effectively and more enjoyably.

REFERENCES

Abilene Christian University. (2008). *ACU connected: Mobile learning.* Retrieved June 19, 2008, from http://www.acu.edu/technology/mobilelearning/index.html.

Abrahamson, L. (2006). A brief history of network classrooms: Effects, cases, pedagogy, and implications. In D. A. Banks (Ed.), *Audience response systems in higher education: Applications and cases.* Hershey, PA: Information Science Publishing.

Anderson, C. (2004). The long tail. *Wired, 12*(10).

Anderson, L. W., & Krathwohl, D. (2001). *A taxonomy for learning, teaching, and assessing: A revision to Bloom's taxonomy of educational objectives.* New York: Longman.

Angelo, T. A., & Cross, P. (1993). *Classroom assessment techniques: A handbook for college teachers.* San Francisco: Jossey-Bass.

Banks, D. A. (Ed.). (2006). *Audience response systems in higher education: Applications and cases.* Hershey, PA: Information Science Publishing.

Barnes, L. B., Christensen, C. R., & Hansen, A. J. (1994). *Teaching and the case method: Text, cases, and readings.* Boston: Harvard Business School Press.

Barnett, J. (2006). Implementation of personal response units in very large lecture classes: Student perceptions. *Australasian Journal of Educational Technology, 22*(4), 474–494.

Beatty, I. D., Gerace, W. J., Leonard, W. J., & Dufresne, R. J. (2006). Designing effective questions for classroom response system teaching. *American Journal of Physics, 74*(1), 31–39.

Beatty, I. D., Leonard, W. J., Gerace, W. J., & Dufresne, R. J. (2006). Question driven instruction: Teaching science (well) with an audience response system. In D. A. Banks (Ed.), *Audience response systems in higher education: Applications and cases.* Hershey, PA: Information Science Publishing.

Belenky, M. F., Clinchy, B. M., Goldberger, N. R., & Tarule, J. M. (1986). *Women's ways of knowing: The development of self, voice, and mind.* New York: Basic Books.

Bombaro, C. (2007). Using audience response technology to teach academic integrity: "The seven deadly sins of plagiarism" at Dickinson College. *Reference Services Review*, *35*(2), 296–309.

Bransford, J. D., Brown, A. L., & Cocking, R. R. (Eds.). (2000). *How people learn: Brain, mind, experience, and school*. Washington, DC: National Academies Press.

Brickman, P. (2006). The Case of the Druid Dracula: A directed "clicker" case study on DNA fingerprinting. *Journal of College Science Teaching*, *36*(2), 48–53.

Briggs, L. (2008, March 26). Ten tips for injecting new technology into your campus. *Campus Technology*.

Bruff, D. (2007). Clickers: A classroom innovation. *National Education Association Advocate*, *25*(1), 5–8.

Bunce, D. M., VandenPlas, J., & Havanki, K. (2006). Comparing the effectiveness on student achievement of a student response system versus online WebCT quizzes. *Journal of Chemical Education*, *83*(3), 488–493.

Caldwell, J. E. (2007). Clickers in the large classroom: Current research and best-practice tips. *Life Sciences Education*, *6*(1), 9–20.

Caron, P. L., & Gely, R. (2004). Taking back the law school classroom: Using technology to foster active student learning. *Journal of Legal Education*, *54*, 551–569.

Case, S. M., & Swanson, D. B. (2002). *Constructing written test questions for the basic and clinical sciences*. Philadelphia: National Board of Medical Examiners.

Cheung, S. L. (2008). Using mobile phone messaging as a response medium in classroom experiments. *Journal of Economic Education*, *39*(1), 51–67.

Cleary, A. M. (2008). Using wireless response systems to replicate behavioral research findings in the classroom. *Teaching of Psychology*, *35*(1), 42–44.

Crouch, C. H., & Mazur, E. (2001). Peer instruction: Ten years of experience and results. *American Journal of Physics*, *69*(9), 970–977.

Deal, A. (2007). *Classroom response systems: A Teaching with Technology White Paper*. Retrieved June 21, 2008, from http://www.cmu.edu/teaching/resources/PublicationsArchives/StudiesWhitepapers/ClassroomResponse_Nov07.pdf.

Draper, S. W., & Brown, M. I. (2004). Increasing interactivity in lectures using an electronic voting system. *Journal of Computer Assisted Learning*, *20*(2), 81–94.

Duch, B., Gron, S., & Allen, D. (2001). *The power of problem-based learning: A practical "how to" for teaching undergraduate courses in any discipline*. Sterling, VA: Stylus.

Ellis, A. B., Cappellari, A., Lisensky, G. C., Lorenz, J. K., Meeker, K., Moore, D., et al. (2000). *Chemistry ConcepTests.* Retrieved June 15, 2008, from http://jchemed.chem.wisc.edu/JCEDLib/QBank/collection/ConcepTests/.

Fagen, A. P., Crouch, C. H., & Mazur, E. (2002). Peer instruction: Results from a range of classrooms. *Physics Teacher, 40*(4), 206–209.

Fies, C., & Marshall, J. (2006). Classroom response systems: A review of the literature. *Journal of Science Education and Technology, 15*(1), 101–109.

Freeman, M., Bell, A., Comerton-Forder, C., Pickering J., & Blayney, P. (2007). Factors affecting educational innovation within class electronic response systems. *Australasian Journal of Educational Technology, 23*(2), 149–170.

Freeman, M., Blayney, P., & Ginns, P. (2006). Anonymity and in class learning: The case for electronic response systems. *Australasian Journal of Educational Technology, 22*(4), 568–580.

Graham, C. R., Tripp, T. R., Seawright, L., & Joeckel, G. L. (2007). Empowering or compelling reluctant participators using audience response systems. *Active Learning in Higher Education, 8*(3), 233–258.

Green P. (n.d.). *ConcepTests for introductory undergraduate astronomy.* Retrieved June 15, 2008, from http://hea-www.harvard.edu/~pgreen/educ/ConcepTests.html.

Hake, R. R. (1998). Interactive-engagement vs. traditional methods: A six-thousand-student survey of mechanics test data for introductory physics courses. *American Journal of Physics, 66*, 64–74.

Hartley, J., & Davies, I. K. (1978). Some observations on the efficiency of lecturing. *Educational Review, 20*, 30–37.

Herreid, C. F. (2006). "Clicker" cases: Introducing case study teaching into large classrooms. *Journal of College Science Teaching, 36*(2), 43–47.

Herreid, C. F. (Ed.). (2007). *Start with a story: The case study method of teaching college science.* Arlington, VA: National Science Teachers Association Press.

Hestenes, D., Wells, M., & Swackhamer, G. (1992). Force concept inventory. *Physics Teacher, 30*, 141–158.

Hinde, K., & Hunt, A. (2006). Using the personal response system to enhance student learning: Some evidence from teaching economics. In D. A. Banks (Ed.), *Audience response systems in higher education: Applications and cases.* Hershey, PA: Information Science Publishing.

Jenkins, A. (2007). Technique and technology: Electronic voting systems in an English literature lecture. *Pedagogy, 7*(3), 526–533.

Judson, E., & Sawada, D. (2002). Learning from past and present: Electronic response systems in college lecture halls. *Journal of Computers in Mathematics and Science Teaching*, *21*(2), 167–181.

Judson, E., & Sawada, D. (2006). Audience response systems: Insipid contrivances or inspiring tools? In D. A. Banks (Ed.), *Audience response systems in higher education: Applications and cases*. Hershey, PA: Information Science Publishing.

Kaleta, R., & Joosten, T. (2007). *Student response systems: A University of Wisconsin study of clickers*. Retrieved June 15, 2008, from http://www.blog.utoronto.ca/in_the_loop/files/ClickersERB0710.pdf.

Klein, S. S., & Harris, A. H. (2007). A user's guide for the legacy cycle. *Journal of Education and Human Development*, *1*(1).

Len, P. M. (2007). Different reward structures to motivate student interaction with electronic response systems in astronomy. *Astronomy Education Review*, *5*(2), 5–15.

Lucas, A. (2007). *Using peer instruction and i-clickers to enhance student participation in calculus*. Retrieved June 12, 2008, from http://www.dillgroup.ucsf.edu/~alucas/iclicker_paper_final.pdf.

Lyman, F. (1981). The responsive classroom discussion. In A. S. Anderson (Ed.), *Mainstreaming digest*. College Park, MD: University of Maryland College of Education.

MacGeorge, E. L., Homan, S. R., Dunning, J. B., Elmore, D., Bodie, G. D., Khichadia, S., et al. (2007). Student evaluation of audience response technology in large lecture classes. *Educational Technology Research and Development*, *56*, 125–145.

Mazur, E. (1997). *Peer instruction: A user's manual*. Upper Saddle River, NJ: Prentice Hall.

McKinney, K. (2007). *Enhancing learning through the scholarship of teaching and learning: The challenges and joys of juggling*. San Francisco: Jossey-Bass.

Merrow, J. (Host). (2007, January 30). College teaching [Podcast]. *The Merrow report*. Public Broadcasting Service. Retrieved June 12, 2008, from PBS.com.

Merrow, J., & Tulenko, J. D. (Producers). (2005). *Declining by degrees: Higher education at risk* [Motion picture]. Alexandria, VA: PBS Home Video.

Michaelsen, L. K., Knight, A. B., & Fink, L. D. (Eds.). (2004). *Team-based learning: A transformative use of small groups in college teaching*. Sterling, VA: Stylus.

Middendorf, J., & Kalish, A. (1996). The "change-up" in lectures. *National Teaching and Learning Forum*, *5*(2), 1–5.

Nagy-Shadman, E., & Desrochers, C. (2008). Student response technology: Empirically grounded or just a gimmick? *International Journal of Science Education*, 1–44, iFirst Article.

Nuhfer, E. (2003). The knowledge survey: A tool for all reasons. *To Improve the Academy, 21,* 59–78.

Penuel, W. R., Boscardin, C. K., Masyn, K., & Crawford, V. M. (2007). Teaching with student response systems in elementary and secondary education settings: A survey study. *Educational Technology, Research and Development, 55*(4), 315–346.

Perry, W. G. (1999). *Forms of ethical and intellectual development in the college years: A scheme.* San Francisco: Jossey-Bass. (Original work published 1968.)

Pollock, S. (n.d.) *Collection of concept tests from CU Boulder.* Retrieved June 12, 2008, from http://www.colorado.edu/physics/EducationIssues/cts.

Roschelle, J., Penuel, W. R., & Abrahamson, L. (2004). *Classroom response and communication systems: Research review and theory.* Paper presented at the Annual Meeting of the American Educational Research Association, San Diego, CA.

Schwartz, D. L., & Bransford, J. D. (1998). A time for telling. *Cognition and Instruction, 16*(4), 475–522.

Science Education Resource Center at Carleton College. (2008). *Conceptsamples.* Retrieved June 15, 2008, from http://serc.carleton.edu/introgeo/interactive/ctestexm.html.

Scornavacca, E., & Marshall, S. (2007). *TXT-2-LRN: Improving students' learning experience in the classroom through interactive SMS.* Paper presented at the 40th Hawaii International Conference on System Sciences. Retrieved June 21, 2008, from http://ieeexplore.ieee.org/iel5/4076361/4076362/04076380.pdf.

Simpson, V., & Oliver, M. (2007). Electronic voting systems for lectures then and now: A comparison of research and practice. *Australasian Journal of Educational Technology, 23*(2), 187–208.

Slater, T. (2005, April). *Ten guaranteed ways to decimate a perfectly good lecture.* Paper presented at the Vanderbilt University Center for Teaching Conversations on Teaching Series, Nashville, TN.

Stowell, J. R., & Nelson, J. M. (2007). Benefits of electronic audience response systems on student participation, learning, and emotion. *Teaching of Psychology, 34*(4), 253–258.

Stuart, S.A.J., Brown, M. I., & Draper, S. W. (2004). Using an electronic voting system in logic lectures: One practitioner's application. *Journal of Computer Assisted Learning, 20*(2), 95–102.

Terrell, M. (n.d.) *GoodQuestions project*. Retrieved June 14, 2008, from http://www.math.cornell.edu/~GoodQuestions/.

Trees, A. R., & Jackson, M. H. (2007). The learning environment in clicker classrooms: Student processes of learning and involvement in large university-level courses using student response systems. *Learning, Media, and Technology, 32*(1), 21–40.

Tversky, A., & Kahneman, D. (1982). Judgments of and by representativeness. In D. Kahneman, P. Slovic, & A. Tversky (Eds.), *Judgment under uncertainty: Heuristics and biases*. Cambridge: Cambridge University Press.

Twetten, J., Smith M. K., Julius, J., & Murphy-Boyer, L. (2007). Successful clicker standardization. *EDUCAUSE Quarterly, 30*(4), 63–67.

Wiggins, G., & McTighe, J. (2005). *Understanding by design* (2nd ed.). Alexandria, VA: Association for Supervision and Curriculum Development.

Wilson, K., & Korn, J. H. (2007). Attention during lectures: Beyond ten minutes. *Teaching of Psychology, 34*(2), 85–89.

Zhu, E. (2007). *Teaching with clickers*. Retrieved June 21, 2008, from http://www.crlt.umich.edu/publinks/CRLT_no22.pdf.

Zullo, H., Parker, M., & Cline, K. (2008). *Project Math QUEST: Math questions to engage students*. Retrieved June 15, 2008, from http://mathquest.carroll.edu/.

Index

75–86; and critical thinking
questions, 86–96; and free-response
questions, 96–98; and recall
questions, 73–80
Contingent teaching, 39
Cornell University, 75; Department of
Mathematics, 76
Cosby, Teresa, 42, 159
Cost factors, 166
Crawford, V. M., xiv, 5
Crider, Anthony, 16, 21, 49, 94, 148, 158,
204
Critical thinking questions, 86–96
Cross, P., 43–44
Crouch, C. H., 17, 114
Cullingford, Elizabeth, 67, 86, 88, 198

D

Darwin, C., 76
Davies, I. K., 34
Day After Tomorrow, The (movie), 44
Deal, A., 185
Delivery modes, 169–171
Desrochers, C., 130, 189, 191
Desrochers, Marcie, 189, 191
Dickinson College, 82
Disciplinary experts, 119
Dorsher, Michael, 6–10
Draper, S. W., 39, 127
Dripps, Weston, 44, 45, 187, 204
Duch, B., 95
Dufresne, R. J., 3, 14, 39, 61, 125, 146
Dunning, J. B., 130

E

Electronic voting systems, 4–5
Ellis, A. B., 118
Elmore, D., 130
Elon University (North Carolina), 16, 21,
49, 86, 94, 101, 148, 158, 201, 204
Engagement, 6
Estrada-Belli, Francisco, 92, 93, 121
Exams, 68–69

F

Fagen, A. P., 17
Fassihi, Parvanak, 17, 18
Feedback, frequent, 202–204
Fies, C., 5
Fink, L. D., 18
Fitzpatrick, Brian, 160

Force Concept Inventory, 122
Formative assessment, 39; defined, 41;
occasions for, using clickers, 43–47
Free-response questions, 96–98
Freeman, M., 177, 186
Fun, classroom: and mathematics case
study, 36–37; using clickers to make
classes, 37–38
Furman University, 42, 44, 159, 187, 204;
Earth and Environment Sciences, 45

G

Gely, Rafael, 80, 81, 99, 100, 200, 203
Gerace, W. J., 3, 14, 39, 61, 125, 146
Ginns, P., 186
Glasgow University, 84
Goldberger, N. R., 93, 133
GoodQuestions Project (Cornell
University Department of
Mathematics), 75, 76
Grading, 130–157, 175–177
Graduate Record Examinations, 71
Graham, C. R., 130, 184
Green, P., 118
Gron, S., 95
Group response systems, 4–5

H

Hake, R. R., 190
Hamlet (Shakespeare), 86–88
Hand-raising method, 186–187
Hansen, A. J., 33
Hardware, 166–167
Harkins, Charlene, 41, 109, 110, 129,
139, 163, 195, 197
Harris, A. H., 120
Hartley, J., 34
Harvard University, 14, 17; Department
of Physics, 79
Havanki, K., 61, 187
Herreid, C. F., 33
Hessler, Kristen, 22, 81, 82, 141, 148, 149,
202
Hestenes, D, 122
High-tech options, 193–196; and cell
phones, 195–196; and laptops,
193–195
Hill, Bill, 23, 110, 111, 116, 200
Hinde, K., 35, 112
Hoekstra, Angel, 49, 107
Holocaust, 95